THE LEGEND MAKERS

About the Author

Gouri Srivastava is a Reader in Education in the Department of Women's Studies, National Council of Educational Research and Training, New Delhi. She has done her M.A. and M.Phil. with high grade points at Jawaharlal Nehru University. She is a recipient of scholarship from Indian Council of Historical Research (ICHR) and from Indian Council of Social Science Research (ICSSR) for completing her doctoral work. She has published widely in academic journals at the national and international levels. She is the author of Women Who Created History and Women's Higher Education in the 19th Century.

THE LEGEND MAKERS
Some Eminent Muslim Women of India

GOURI SRIVASTAVA

CONCEPT PUBLISHING COMPANY, NEW DELHI-110059

ISBN 81-8069-001-6

First Published 2003

Published and Printed by
Ashok Kumar Mittal
Concept Publishing Company
A/15-16, Commercial Block, Mohan Garden
New Delhi-110059 (India)

Phones: 5351460, 5351794
Fax: 091–(11)–5357103
E-mail: publishing@conceptpub.com

Preface

The present book is a humble attempt in giving a vivid account of the contribution of thirty muslim women in medieval, modern and in the contemporary periods. The manuscript discusses their journey towards attaining their goals in different fields and is a poignant story of their trails and successes which they have portrayed in their biographical works, short stories, poems and in the print and the audio-visual media. Their work has become a great source of motivation not only to the womenfolk of their families but to all the women belonging to different religions, caste and creed. Some of the strategies adopted by them, i.e. opening formal institutions of learning, writing motivational literary work has inspired women till date. Perhaps it has also continued to encourage parents especially from muslim families to send their daughters to formal institutions of learning in the present times.

I am deeply indebted to my parents, my husband and my son Gaurav Prakash who have taken keen interest in my work and have constantly encouraged me. I am also grateful to Dr. Mona Yadav, my colleague at the Department of Women's Studies, N.C.E.R.T. for her support and useful suggestions.

I express my sincere thanks to all the members and staff of the National Archives at Delhi and Bhopal, Nehru Memorial Museum and Library, N.C.E.R.T. library, and the library at the All India Women's Conference.

The views expressed in the book are totally those of the author. I was inspired to undertake this work while I was doing my doctoral work on 'The Study of the Socio-Economic and Political Aspects of the Growth of Higher Education of Women in Bombay Presidency 1857-1921'. This manuscript is a reference material only.

GOURI SRIVASTAVA

Contents

1

Introduction

Islamic religion favoured the education of both boys and girls. Prophet Muhammad had great regard for both men and women of learning. Thus, we find that the early education was open to both boys and girls.

"......The initial education of a Muslim boy and girl began with the bismillah ceremony at the age of four years, four months and four days. The little child was coached in advance and would recite the first verse of the Quran, then would be rewarded with sweets. Thereafter, the child began learning verses of the Quran by heart from a tutor (*Ustad*) who came to the house. Daughters as well as sons learned the Quran in a parrot-like manner, taught either by grey-bearded tutor or by a woman teacher (*Ustani*). After a few years of basic instruction at home, a boy ventured out to a mosque school, or Maktabs, or to the home of a teacher (Maulvi). Higher education was acquired by him in Madrasah".[1]

The Ustanis came to the house to teach older girls, and these women teachers frequently had a limited repertory of literacy skills. Many girls received no education beyond memorization of a few Quranic passages; others learned to read some Arabic during their Quran lessons, and Persian and Urdu from their fathers or brothers. Normally girls at home had little time for other study, as most of their waking hours were devoted for helping their mothers in domestic chores, such as cooking, sewing and looking after their younger brothers and sisters. In this way daughters learned from their mothers.

Thus, girls' were domestically educated. Despite, higher education not being common among girls, we find that few Muslim women in the medieval period (i.e. Sultanate and the Mughal period) were great rulers, administrators, social reformers, writers and poets.

The Mughal emperor always took great care about the education of their daughters. The daughters of Shahjahan and Aurangzeb were educated and talented ladies. Not only this, they took active part in contemporary politics. Shahjahan's daughter Jahanara Begam and Roshanara Begam were highly educated and accomplished ladies. The daughters of Aurangzeb also possessed literary taste. His eldest daughter Zeb-un-Nissa was very proficient in academic field. His daughter Zinat-un-Nissa was also a lady of literary pursuits.

The above mentioned women have left their mark not only to the period they belonged to but became a source of inspiration to other women of their times and also to those of the subsequent periods. Their examples were richly emulated by muslim women of the 19th and 20th century. These women of the 19th and 20th century owed their education to their fathers, brothers, husbands who belonged to the educated social reformist class. They wanted to cducate their women so that they become good companions and enlightened mothers of their children.

In the history of women's education, especially formal education, the above mentioned century is very important as it saw the rise of an educated middle class or the intelligentsia who constituted both Hindus and Muslims. They were greatly influenced by the western system of education and the values upheld by it, i.e. liberalism, rationality equality and so on.

These educated classes or the bhadralok began examining the Indian society critically and wanted to study those factors that retarded its social progress. Nearly all of them came to a common conclusion that the existing social customs and traditions that were derogatory to women were the chief factors that was responsible in inhibiting social change and keeping the societal clock backward. There was a sincere urge on their part to question the existing customs and traditions and undo them by drawing parallel examples from religious texts which accorded high or complementary status to women along with men. Religious texts were read and re-read and almost all the Hindu reformers agreed that the Rig-Vedic period was one where women enjoyed a better social status. In fact, customs and traditions did not have an adverse effect on the status of women. It was only during the later Vedic and Brahmanical period that the status of women gradually deteriorated. The customs and traditions that relegated the position of women in society were – child marriage, purdah, enforced widowhood and finally, the practice of sati (or physical immolation) that enveloped the entire mortal existence of women from birth to adulthood. Among the above mentioned customs it was child marriage and to some extent purdah that was commonly practiced among Hindus and Muslims. Further, these prevalent customs had a significant bearing on the education of Hindu and Muslim women. The marriage ceremony of Hindus and Muslim girls normally took place before she attained puberty. This prevented her from attending formal institutions of learning. The pathshalas (primary) and the tols (higher centre of brahmanical learning), Maktabs (primary) and Madrasa (higher centre of Muslim education) were devoid of female students. Also, certain myths and notional beliefs that were equally shared by Hindus and Muslim parents regarding the education of their daughters were as follows:

— Girls needed no formal guidance because household chores – i.e. cooking, stitching, housekeeping could be learnt through practice and guidance from senior female members of the family.
— Education would lead to early widowhood.
— Reading and writing of girls in the long run would violate rules of purdah.

In fact, the protection of a girls chastity, and hence the family's *izzat* or honour was definitely more important than development of her mind.

Role of the Educated Hindu and Muslim Intelligentsia in Promoting Girls' Education

Initially the educated Hindu intelligentsia like Raja Ram Mohan Roy,

Ishwar Chand Vidyasagar, Ranade, Gopal Hari Deshmukh, Justice Telang B. Malabari, Maharishi Karve and host of others were strongly against the above mentioned customs and prevalent notional beliefs and myths. In their own way they sought to improve the status of women either through social legislation, or setting personal examples, e.g. Maharishi Karve, a great social reformer in Bombay Presidency, married a widow. Some of them also opened formal institutions of learning for girls. Few of them wrote in journals and magazines advocating the cause of women's education. There was a strong realization on their part that only education would instil confidence in women, enable them to have a questioning attitude and in the long run prevent them from submitting to irrational customs and traditions.

While the Hindu social reformers were trying different ways and methods in improving the status of women, the Muslim intelligentsia and reformers were initially slow to respond. They were apprehensive about the western system of education and values upheld by it, but gradually men from the middle and upper middle class began acquiring the English system of education and the ideas and values that were upheld by it. Some of the eminent Muslim social reformers were Sir Syed Ahmad Khan, Sheikh Abdullah and Maulana Hali. Sir Syed Ahmad Khan though was a strong supporter of western education for men but as far as women were concerned he was reluctant. He felt that home learning needed no formal guidance. Further women's education would arouse a lot of opposition from the orthodox section of society particularly the Mullas. His own mother Azizunnissa Begam was not formally instructed, but was well-versed in Quran and had elementary knowledge of Persian. In 1875, Sir Syed Ahmad established the Mohammedan Anglo-Oriental College which was only for men.

Strategies Used by the Reformers for Promoting Education of the Muslim Girls

Unlike Sir Syed Ahmad there were some Muslim social reformers who were genuinely concerned about the education of women. Like the Hindu social reformers they were of the view that education would instil confidence among women and empower them to play the role of prime agent of socialization effectively (i.e. as wives, mothers and so on). They also drew parallel from their religion which clearly stated that :

> "The ink of the scholar is more holy than the blood of the martyr."

In fact, Islam promoted education of both men and women. Picking up this positive phenomena from their religion along with their deep faith in western ideas and beliefs, some of the reformers, like Sheikh Abdullah (of Aligarh) and Maulana Hali opened formal institutions for Muslim girls. Maulana Hali started a small primary school for the daughter of his family and his friend in Panipat around 1894. Similarly, Sheikh Abdullah started a girls' school in Aligarh in 1906. The other pioneers who opened institution for formal education of girls were Maulana Karamat Hussain and the Maharaja of Mahmudabad, who founded the Muslim Girls' School in Lucknow in 1912.

The curriculum in most of the formal primary Muslim girls' schools consisted of Urdu reading and (sometimes) writings, arithmetic, the Quran and needlework. Sometimes in girls' secondary school, science courses were replaced by domestic science, cooking, sewing, childcare hygiene and other practical household skills. Girls' schools that were specifically Muslim gave some religious instruction – the Quran, diniyat (theology), the life of the Prophet and of exemplary Islamic women; they also required regular daily prayer, and for older girls, fasting during the month of Ramadhan. There were variations in the curricular themes but the schools that were opened by the reformers combined the instruction of the three R's, religious instruction and practical household skills that would enable girls to become efficient managers of their houses. It would also help them to become good mothers, wives and sisters.

Most of the formal schools that were opened by the Muslim intelligentsia and social reformers faced certain common problems i.e. – paucity of Muslim women teachers. This was also true for the schools that were established for girls by the Hindu social reformers. Further, Christian teachers were generally avoided because Muslims seemed more afraid of proselytization than any other community at this time. Also, the prevalence of early marriage among Muslim girls did not allow them more than two or three years of schooling. Fierce opposition from orthodox sections of society who strongly felt that sending Muslim girls to school was against all Islamic traditions, effected the attendance of girls in formal institutions of learning that were established by educated Muslim intelligentsia.

Apart from establishing formal institutions of learning the educated Muslim intelligentsia brought out some literature, magazines, periodicals that played a catalytic role in promoting the cause of education of Muslim girls. One of the earliest literary works that became prominent during the 19th century was "Tehzib-I-Niswan", founded by Mumtaz Ali of Lahore and his wife, Mohammadi Begam in 1898. It was weekly published and its main purpose was to provide reading material for women. It gave some world news and directed its readers attention towards rampart social evils of the day. The other significant monthly magazine was the "Khatoon". This was brought out by Sheikh Abdullah of Aligarh in 1904. It was the journal of the women's education section of the All-India Muslim Educational Conference and addressed itself to the Muslim elite. Its main purpose was to advocate the cause among Muslim women by founding local associations to raise funds for opening schools for girls. It also contained, discussions pertaining to the problems of education, for example suitable curricula, and the need for good textbooks. "Khatoon", ceased publication in 1914 after the girls school in Aligarh had been firmly established and Sheikh Abdullah and his wife became totally involved in running the school and the hostel.

Another well-known Urdu monthly magazine was "Ismat" which was published from Delhi. It was founded in 1908 by the well-known Urdu novelist, Rashidul Khairi. "Ismat" was primarily a literary journal which encouraged creative writing among women, but a number of men were also among its contributors and the main thrust of the journal was to promote women's education in order to make them good wives and mothers. Urdu magazines were also published from Bombay and Hyderabad State and most of them catered to the creative urge of Muslim women by publishing their stories, articles and poems. They also focused attention on the disabilities from which women suffered due to ignorance and superstition, the humiliation inflicted on them by polygamy, the sufferings of the child bride and widows and of unequal marriages where young girls were married to men twice and thrice their age. The objectives and ideals of female education were also spelt out. Both men and women believed that the chief aim of education for girls was to get well placed bridegrooms for them – education was meant to develop such womanly virtues as chastity, self-sacrifice, submission, devotion, kindness and patience.

Government Role in Promoting Girls Education

It is significant to note that unlike the male intelligentsia and the social reformers, who were both Hindus and Muslims, the British Government was late to respond to the issues, concerning women's education. They deliberately avoided the issue because of its sensitive nature and also they did not want to intervene in the natives – social and religious issues. It was only in 1854 that Wood's Educational Despatch reflected government's concern for promoting women's education. The despatch noted the increased demand on the part of many Indians to educate their daughters, and urged support for all efforts to promote female education. In fact, the system of grant-in-aid was clearly mentioned in the Despatch to assist the indigenous educational endeavours.

Governmental efforts led to the overall expansion of girls' education. We find that by the early 20th century the number of girl schools and the number of students in them had grown apace, a trend that accelerated after World War I. In 1929 the Hartog Committee issued a detailed study of the state of education in British India, with chapters on women's education and on Muslim education in particular. The committee's report provides a convenient statistical compendium with which to assess the growth of girls' education.[2]

Table 1 : Growth of Girls Education (1917–1927)

Province	1917 Girls	1917 Students	1927 Girls	1927 Students	1927 Students as % of female pop. of school age	1927 Students as % of total female pop.
U.P.	1,236	63,286	1,845	19,215	3.9	0.5
Punjab	1,030	54,901	1,388	89,517	5.7	0.8
Bengal	9,566	289,800	14,780	416,415	13.1	1.8
Bombay	1,216	134,684	1,666	215,859	16.8	2.3
Madras	1,815	307,125	3,579	525,697	17.9	2.5

Source: Hartog Committee Report, pp. 146-147.

The above table gives an account of only formal institutions taking no account of informal or home-based, "zenana" education which was initially promoted by the Christian missionaries. Nor are they broken down according to religion. In fact, it is difficult to get a clear picture regarding the status of Muslim women's education. The table gives an idea that in the three Presidencies of Bengal, Bombay and Madras, girls' education was ahead than in U.P. and Punjab.[3]

The committee's data on the education of Muslims is given below :

Table 2 : Education of Muslim Students

Province	Muslims in population %	Muslims in student population %
U.P.	14.3	18.1
Punjab	55.3	50.0
Bengal	54.0	51.3
Bombay (minus Sind)	8.6	13.8
Madras	6.7	11.0

Source: Hartog Committee Report, pp. 190-193.

Table 2 does not give a picture on the educational status of girls in the above province. In other words the data is not gender dis-aggregated.

The Hartog Committee noted that in provinces where Muslims were in a minority, they consistently had a higher percentage in school than their percentage in the population, whereas in Punjab and Bengal, they were slightly in majority, their percentage in school was proportionately less. The Committee also observed a significant increase in Muslim education in Punjab in the decade between 1917 and 1927, and further noted that the percentage of Muslims among girl students in Punjab was fairly high: 26 per cent overall, 17 per cent at the middle level and 15 per cent of women college students.

Thus, the combined efforts of the male intelligentsia and the British Government led to the overall expansion of formal education of Muslim girls' in the 19th and 20th century. However their effort was like a drop in the ocean. Muslim women who received formal education constituted a microscopic minority and largely belonged to the urban educated families.

Role of the Muslim Women Intelligentsia

The above mentioned fortunate educated women questioned the institution of purdah (symbol of segregation) and gave it up in most of the cases. In their own individual capacity they opened social organizations and formal institutions of learning for Muslim girls. Some of them crossed the inhibited terrain of reading and writing and wrote books, contributed articles in magazines and journals. The literary work of these educated Muslim women mirrors the status of women in general in the 19th and 20th century. Their work also motivated women to question the existing custom and traditions that were particularly derogatory to the overall status of women. It also encouraged women particularly Muslim women, to take to education. One of the earliest social organizations established by educated women was the All India Muslim Ladies Conference which was convened by the Begams of Bhopal at Aligarh in 1915. In 1917 this Conference was held at Lahore, and a resolution was passed against polygamy. It is significant to note that there was a storm of protest by Muslim men. Even Rashidul Khairi one of the most prolific and popular urdu novelists of the early twentieth century, and the founder of the earliest urdu literary magazine for women, Ismat, that he began publishing in Delhi in 1908, condemned the resolution. This was a shock to his women reader. He had attacked polygamy in many of his novels and articles and his writings overflowed with sympathy for the sad plight of Muslim women, but he was uncomfortable at the thought of women demanding their own rights. He was a true patriarch at the heart and strongly believed that men must be the reformers of society and not women themselves.

The other significant organization that came up during the period was the Hyderabad Ladies' Association founded in 1902 by Begum Khedive Jung, the first woman graduate of Hyderabad. There was an "Anjuman-I-Khawateen Islam" established in Lahore around 1906. Its meetings were held in the house of Sir Mohammad Shafi, to discuss and formulate proposals for the spread of education and social reform and securing rights given to women by Islam.

Apart from establishing social organization that took up the cause of uplifting the status of women some of the educated Muslim women established formal institutions of learning. In Bengal Presidency the initial move was begun by Nawab Faizunnessa Chaudhurani. In 1901 she founded an English middle school named after her daughter, Badrunnessa. She also set up primary schools at each of her administrative centres (Racharis) in her estate. Perhaps her single greatest achievement was the establishment of an English-medium school for girls in 1873. The Faizunnessa Girl's Pilot High School was designed for pardanashin girls. Faizunnessa Girls' School was assisted in her efforts by Kalicharan De, the famous Brahmo leader of Comilla. A hostel was subsequently added to the school. Many women who later became eminent studied in this school, though the initial response from the Muslim community was lukewarm. It was later taken up by the government and converted into a high school. Faizunnessa may therefore be regarded as the pioneer in Muslim women's education in Bengal. The other significant women who took up the cause of women's education was Rokeya Sakhawat Hossein (1880-1932). She founded the Sakhawat Memorial School in 1911 at Calcutta. This was her single great achievement because the school was an integral part of her ceaseless campaign for the education of Muslim girls and their journey out of the "abarodh". No one before or after her had worked so tirelessly for the cause. At first the medium of instruction was Urdu. This clearly reflects the pro-Urdu culture of the Sharif (upper or aristocratic) families of Bengal at that time. Their first formal lessons under the syllabus of the school were conducted in Urdu.

As a result of the activities of the male and female intelligentsia Muslim girls started enrolling themselves in formal institution of learning in Bengal Presidency. Census figures for the year 1881 reveal that the number of female students at the primary level during 1881-82 was around 17,000 in Bengal, of whom 8.9 per cent were Muslim. The figure rose to almost 58,000 in 1901-02 of whom 10.9 per cent were Muslim. In 1931-32 the number increased to 5,35,000 of whom an amazing 56.5 per cent were again Muslim. The attendance of Muslim girls was greater at the primary level but declined steadily at the middle and higher levels. In the 19th century Muslim girls in Bengal Presidency had some access to traditional educational institutions such as maktabs, but they mainly imparted religious education. From the late 19th century onwards there was a move towards growing secularization of the curricula at these schools initiated by the government. Before 1906 there were three high schools for girls in East Bengal. Eden in Dhaka, Khastagir in Chittagong and Alexander in Mymensingh. It is significant to note that Bethune School did not admit Muslim girls as late as 1895. The traditional obstacles to female education still persisted – purdah, early marriage, lack of material facilities and government patronage, the rigid orthodoxy of the Muslims compared to the Hindu and Brahmo communities and the lack of trained female teachers.[4]

Educational schemes for Muslim women received fresh impetus after the partition of Bengal in 1905, due to increased government patronage and heightened awareness within the community. In fact, the new provincial government wanted to do all in its power to encourage female education by affording guidance and assistance on practical lines.

During the same period we find that in the Princely State of Bhopal, the Begam actively took up the cause of female education. Like the Bengal Presidency they established formal institution of learning for Muslim girls. Nawab Sultan Jahan Begam, the last Nawab in the female lineage, opened a new institution, called the Sultania Girls School. This school was opened in an annexe of the Taj Mahal in Bhopal. The school was primarily meant for girls belonging to noble families. A closed conveyance was provided by the state to bring all the girls to the school in the morning and to take them back in the afternoon. In 1912, the Sultania Girls School was affiliated with the middle school course of the University of Allahabad.

The other significant school opened by the Begam was called the Victoria School for girls. It is significant to note that both these schools continue to exist even to this day. A special school for Hindu girls was opened in 1907. This school was named as Birjisia Kanya Pathshala.

A school for widows and destitute women was also established to teach them some useful professions, mainly needlework so that they may be able to earn an independent living to keep up their self-respect.

In one of her writings Nawab Sultan Jahan Begam stated that, "Education to my mind, is the best ornament of a woman".[5] She further stated that, "It is perhaps forgotten that women, too, are half the community, and no real progress can be achieved if the educational needs of this important area is neglected and starved off."[6]

In fact, Nawab Sultan Jahan Begam's vision of female education was to give training to mature girls to be able to be good mothers and housewives.

Some of the educated Muslim women were prolific writers. They expressed their creative urge by publishing their own stories, articles and poems. In their own writings they tried to focus attention on the disabilities from which women suffered due to ignorance and superstition, the humiliation inflicted on them by polygamy, the sufferings of child brides and widows and of unequal marriages where the young girls were married to men twice and thrice their age. The objectives and ideals of female education were also spelt out. Both men and women believed that the chief aim of education for the girls was to get well placed bridegrooms for them – education was meant to develop such womanly virtues as chastity, self-sacrifice, submission, devotion, kindness and patience.

Some of the well-known writers were – Bint Nazrul Baqar. She grew up in Sialkot, Punjab in 1890 in a Shi'a family that maintained a tradition of women's literacy. Her father, Sayyid Muhammad Nazrul Baqar was a military supplier and his sister Akbari Begam, wrote one of the earliest Urdu novels. Bint Nazer was among the first subscriber to Tahzib un-Niswan. She contributed short articles very frequently and began to be known as 'tahzibi behin' the sisterhood of readers of the journal. She became such a regular contributor that, in 1910, when Mumtaz Ali decided to start a publication specifically for girls, *Phul* (flower), he asked Bint Nazer to become its editor. This she did for several years, until her marriage. She also wrote a story entitled, *Voh Ankhen* (Those Eyes).

Rashid Jahan another significant literary figure (1905-52) made a mark in the learned circle. She was the daughter of Shaikh Abdullah of Aligarh and Wahid Jahan Begam. She grew up in a home where all the women were involved in educational and literary pursuits. Her mother and aunt taught at the Aligarh Girls' School and wrote for Urdu magazine, including their own journal, *Khatun*. Rashid Jahan became a doctor in her later life and an author. Two of her outstanding contributions to the volume are *Dilli Ki Sair* (A Visit to Delhi) and *Parde Ke Piche* (Behind the Veil), portray women's plight with great economy and irony. The author sought to set a new trend in literature, away from sentimental language, romantic situations and upper-class character, towards addressing problems of social inequity and life among the oppressed, including labourer and women.

Rashid Jahan's work inspired Ismat Chughtai, who later became one of the best-known authors of modern Urdu short stories. The most controversial work produced by her was *Lihaf* (The Quilt) that appeared in *Adub-I-Lutif* in 1942. *Lihaf* caused a lot of furor, for it was a frank treatment, not only of a wife's sexual frustration, but also that of a woman's relationship with a female servant with whom she finds emotional and sexual companionship.

In Bengal Presidency the first woman to write in modern prose was Bibi Taherunnessa. Her essay in the form of a long letter, *Bamaganer Rachana* appeared in the *Bamabodhini Patrika* (February-March, 1864). In her essay, Taherunnessa pleads for women's education. However, the credit for being the first Bengali Muslim woman in modern times to write a full-length book goes to Nawab Faizunnessa Chaudhurani, the author of *Rupjalal*. It was published from Dhaka in 1876. It is significant to note that even before Faizunnessa's works were discovered, Rokeya Sakhawat Hossein was usually hailed as the first Muslim female writer of modern times. Rokeya started her literary career in 1901 when her essay *Pipasha* (The Thirst) appeared in *Nabaprabha*. Her next piece *'Alankarna Badge of Slavery'* (Jewellery or Badge of Slavery) created a stir. It was published in the journal *Mahila* edited by Girish Chandra Sen from Calcutta. Though Rokeya's feminism is woven into most of her writings, there are some pieces, which are especially concerned with problems of women. Into this category fall *Stree Jatin Abanati* (1905), *Ardhangi* (1905) and *Narin Adhikar* (Women's Rights) her last work, published posthumously. Rokeya's only novel *Padmarg* (1924) is a narration of life in Tarini Bhavan, a sanctuary where women of all creeds have found refuge and live a life of dignity.

Shamsunnahar was another women writer who contributed in enriching Bengali language and literature. Her writings mainly deal with various aspects of education in Bengal (primary education, Bengali Muslim women's education, etc.). In 1933, Nahar and her brother Habibullah Bahar jointly brought out the progressive periodical '*Bulbul*' from Calcutta.

Razia Khatun Chaudhurani (1907-34) during her brief life, made a name as an essayist, poet and a short story writer. She wrote a book entitled '*Sramik*'.

Thus, educated Muslim *bhadramahilas* or (educated Muslim women), though a handful in the above mentioned period, successfully established schools, wrote their own biographical account, poems and short stories that became a source of inspiration and motivation to young and old women. Further, their individual examples of giving up of purdah and taking up higher education was emulated by the urban Muslim women of the 19th and 20th century. They embarked on literary and, later, other careers, and their desire for education intensified.

In the proposed manuscript a humble attempt has been made to identify eminent Muslim women who have left their mark in different fields since the medieval period.

NOTES

1. Law, N.N., *Promotion of Learning in India*, p. 128.

   Rawat, P.L., *History of Indian Education*, p. 90.

   Minault, Gail, *Secluded Scholars: Women's Education and Muslim Social Reform in Colonial India*, Oxford University Press, New Delhi, 1998, p. 19.
2. Indian Statutory (Simon) Commission, *Report of the Educational Sub-Committee* (Hartog Committee), London, 1929, pp. 146-147.
3. *Ibid.*, pp. 190-193.
4. Amin, Nishat Sonia, *"The Early Muslim Bhadramahila: The Growth of Learning and Creativity 1876 to 1939"*, in *From the Seams of History: Essays on Indian Women* (ed.) by Ray, Bharati, Oxford University Press, Delhi, 1995.
5. Mittal, Kamla, *A History of Bhopal State: Development of Constitution.*
6. *Ibid.*

2

Razia Sultan

(1236—1240)

Razia Sultan was the daughter of Iltutmish, who was a great ruler of Delhi Sultanate. She had the unique distinction of being the only woman who occupied the throne of Delhi. Her father, Iltutmish, was aware of her capabilities and is said to have formally nominated her as his successor, after his Gwalior campaign. He stuck to his decision in spite of the vigorous protest of his proud nobles, who were not happy with the idea of having a woman as their sovereign ruler.

Razia possessed all qualities of a good administrator. She was well-versed in the reading of the *Quran*, and had a fair knowledge of several other sciences. She had given ample proof of her dauntless courage by accompanying her father in several campaigns. "The men of discernment," remarks Firishta, "could find no defect in her except that she was created in the form of a woman." One of the contemporary historian, Minaj-us-Siraj, stated that, "she was a great monarch, wise, just, generous, benefactor to her realm, a dispenser of equity, the protector of her people, and leader of her armies."

It is significant to note that after the death of Iltutmish in 1236, the Turkish nobles, disregarded his wishes and set up one of his sons, Ruknuddin Firuz Shah on the throne. While Ruknuddin Firuz was busy in sensual pursuits, the affairs of the state were looked after by his mother Shah Tukran. She was a very ambitious lady, who tried to get rid of all those nobles who were against him by degrading some and murdering others. And attempt was made even to take the life of Razia Sultana.

This high handed on the part of Shah Tukran provoked the wrath of the nobles, who, repenting of their folly, revolted against Ruknuddin and proclaimed Razia as the Sultan of Delhi.

Razia ascended the throne in A.D. 1236, and casting aside the veil, held court in her father's place. She had a difficult task before her. The Shamsi nobles, whom even Iltutmish could not control with great difficulty, wanted to keep all their power in their own hands. Razia's accession was not recognised by some of them, who also revolted. Undaunted, Razia marched against them. She successfully crushed the rebellion that occurred in Multan, Lahore, and Hansi. Muhammad Junaidi, Wazir of the kingdom, who was one of her greatest opponents was also defeated by her.

After crushing these rebellions she had a comparatively peaceful time and carried on the administration of her vast kingdom with great skill and wisdom. She was aware that for running the administration successfully she had to curb the power of the Turkish nobility, and with this in mind she promoted an Abyssinian slave, Yaqut, to the high office of master of royal stables, showering a lot of favours upon him and setting him up as a rival to the Shamsi nobles. This favour shown to Yaqut was disliked by other nobles. Loyal nobles also turned hostile towards her. Ultimately Turkish nobles in her camp succeeded in putting Malik Yaqut to death. Left without a loyal protector, Razia was now a prisoner in their hands. They took her with them to Bhatinda, confined her in the fort there, reconciled Altuniya, and proclaimed Razia's brother Bahram Shah as Sultan of Delhi. She, however, did not give way to despair yet and won over her captor, Altuniya, to her side. She later married him, and recruiting an army of Khokhars and other zamindars, they marched out together to recapture the lost throne. She and her husband were twice defeated by Malik Jalaluddin Balban, who later became the Sultan of Delhi. Both Altuniya and Razia while fleeing from the battle field were murdered by some zamindar in 1240 A.D.

Thus, ended the short reign of Razia Sultan for three and a half years. Despite her reign being short, she succeeded in restoring the prestige of the Turkish kingdom in India. In fact, she was the first Turkish ruler of Delhi to have imposed the royal will upon the amirs and maliks.

It is usually believed that the cause of Razia's fall was her sex, as the Turkish nobles did not like to be ruled by a woman. But the primary cause of her downfall seems to have been the determined ambition of the Turkish military aristocracy to keep the ruler of Delhi a tool in their hands and to retain the power for themselves, whereas Razia had all through followed the opposite course of making herself supreme in the kingdom and concentrating power in her hands. Her sex was only a secondary cause of her premature end. She lies buried in a part of old Delhi known as Bulbuli Khana.

REFERENCES

Nizami, Khaliq Ahmad, *Some Aspects of Religion and Politics in India During the Thirteenth Century*, Idarah-I-Adabiyat-i-Delli, 1978, Delhi.

Srivastava, A.L., *History of India (1000-1707 A.D.).* Shiva Lal Agarwala & Company, Educational Publishers, Agra.

3

Gulbadan Begam

(1523 — 1603)

Gulbadan Begam was the daughter of the Mughal emperor Babur and his wife Dildar Begam. She received good education in her early days. She later married Khidr Khwaja, and her only daughter Ruqayya Sultan was married to Emperor Akbar. Despite his dissensions, she made a very hazardous pilgrimage to Mecca in 1575, reaching her destination after nearly two years. She stayed in Hijaz for three years and a half, spending large sums in charity, and returned safely to India.

There is no recorded history regarding Gulbadan's education, but there is no doubt that she was a well educated lady. Turkish was her mother tongue and she was proficient in this language. She was well versed in Persian.

Gulbadan Begam has immortalized her name by writing the *Humayun-namah*, a work which has been recognized as the most valuable contemporary records of Humayun's reign. This work of her's has no literary pretensions, being written in simple Persian with a large admixture of Turkish words. Gulbadan possessed considerable poetic talent, but unfortunately her verses have not been preserved.

Mrs. Beveridge quotes one of her couplet from Tazkirat-ul-Khawatin of Mir Mahdi Shirzi, which runs thus—

> *"Har pari ki auha' ashaq khud yar nist, Tu Yaqih midan ki hech az' umr bar-khur-dar hist."*[1]

S.K. Banerji has quoted the verse thus:

> *"The fairy-faced one that is not in love with her lover. Thou mayst be certain, is not happy in life."*[2]

Gulbadan Begam was a woman of literary taste. Her interest in reading and writing shows that she must have possessed a good library of her own. Her love for books is proved by one incident. Bayazid wrote *Humayun Nama* and nine copies were made. Two copies went to the emperor's library, three to the three princes, i.e. Salim, Murad and Danyal, one copy to Gulbadan, two to Abul Fazl and one was kept by the author.[3] Thus, her library was enriched by valuable and rare collections.

She spent her last years in pious devotion and charitable deeds and died at the ripe age of eighty in 1603.[4] Her death was a great loss to Akbar and his mother, for her wisdom and rich experience helped them to solve many knotty problems. The emperor not only accompanied her bier but carried it on his shoulders for part of her last journey.[5]

NOTES

1. S.K. Banerji, *Humayun Badshah,* Vol. 11, Maxwell Company, Lucknow, 1941, p. 320.
2. H.N. (Bev.), Introduction, p. 76.
3. *Ibid.*
4. Nath, Renuka, *Notable Mughal and Hindu Women in the 16th and 17th Centuries A.D.*, Inter-India Publications, New Delhi, 1990.
5. Madhavananda, Swami, Majumdar, Ramesh Chandra, *Great Women of India*, Swami Ananyananda, President, Advaita Ashram, Mayavati Pithoragarh, Himalayas, Calcutta, 1982.

4

Chand Bibi

(1547 — 1599)

Chand Bibi was the daughter of Husain Nizam Shah of Ahmadnagar. She was a great scholar in Arabic and Persian language and could also speak several Deccani language fluently. She was later married to Ali Adil Shah of Bijapur. Chand Bibi received the fortress of Sholapur as part of her dowry. This proved a great blessing to her husband. He encouraged her and even recognized her rich talent and even consulted her on all administrative matters. She used to ride with him on horseback, to review the army parades and took an active part in all his military campaigns. In 1580 her husband was treacherously murdered.

After her husbands death, his nephew Ibrahim Adil Shah, a minor, succeeded the throne of Bijapur. In fact Chand Bibi became the regent and the real ruler of this kingdom. As a regent she greatly improved the state administration. She also educated the minor king with great ability and tact.

Chand Bibi had to face a lot of opposition from the amirs who were jealous of her and wanted to overthrow her. One of the amir Kishwar Khan tried to oust her. By a ruse he succeeded in turning some nobles against her, and she was asked to leave Bijapur. On her refusal she was given a rough treatment. She was dragged out of her apartment with the help of a slave girl, was put in a palanquin and carried hurriedly to the fortress of Satara, where she was confined. Gradually the Bijapur nobles realized their folly and set Chand Bibi free. Kishwar Khan was later killed.

Chand Bibi was once again restored to her former position. Now she appointed an Abyssinian amir, Ikhlas Khan, as a minister.

The main reason for appointing him was to counter balance the power of the Deccani nobles. She was not lucky with this choice of hers because he, i.e. Ikhlas Khan resented her partiality to foreigners, specially Afzal Khan Shirazi, and managed by surreptitious means to put him and the brahmin minister Pandit Rasu to death. This naturally enraged Chand Bibi, who got him imprisoned with the help of Ainul Mulk. He was, however, released later, and distinguished himself in several battles against the Qutb Shahis of Golconda.

In spite of the best efforts of Chand Bibi, the affairs in Bijapur and Ahmadnagar greatly deteriorated. This was mainly due to the mutual jealousies and rivalry of the Deccani and Abyssynian amirs. The climax was reached when Ibrahim Nizam Shah, king of Ahmadnagar was killed, and Mian Manjhu, an ambitious amir, defying the wishes of Chand Bibi, set up a young prince, Ahmad Shah on the throne. Chand Bibi now left for Bijapur in disgust. Manjhu, feeling his position insecure, appealed to prince Murad for help, and the latter, marching from his headquarters in Gujarat, promptly appeared before the walls of Ahmadnagar with a large army. Manjhu now realized his mistake and he entreated Chand Bibi to return to Ahmadnagar and rescue it from the Mughal menace, and, in spite of her advanced age and feeble health, she hurried to defend her homeland. She managed to keep prince Murad and his redoubtable general Khan-i-Khanan at bay, and finally compelled them to raise the siege. Once, when a portion of the rampart was blown away by mines laid by the besiegers, she rushed out of her palace barefooted with number of trusted followers, a veil on her face and sword in her hands. She succeeded in repairing the damaged wall overnight Prince Murad was extremely impressed by her valour and courage that he gave her the title of Chand Sultan. He left Ahmadnagar after accepting the province of Berar, as the prize of his campaign.

Internal strifes especially among the nobles in Ahmadnagar continued, this gave an opportunity to Akbar, who was himself camping in Burhanpur, to send an expedition to the unfortunate kingdom, under his son Daniyal and Khan-i-Khanan. Chand Bibi realised that it was impossible to hold out against the mighty army that surrounded her city, she wanted to conclude an honourable peace with prince Daniyal. Fate had other thing in store for her. She was treacherously executed by some of the Deccani amirs in 1599.

Thus, ended the reign of the brave Begam who till the last moment of her life wanted to save her country. During her brief reign she not only administered her province well but also became a great patron of scholars. She also helped foreigners who came to seek fortune in India.

REFERENCE

Madhavananda, Swami, Majumdar, Ramesh Chandra, *Great Women of India*, Published by Swami Ananyananda, President, Advaita Ashrama, Mayavati Pithoragarh, Himalayas, Calcutta, 1982.

5

Nur Jahan Begam

(1577—1646)

In the annals of Mughal history no woman had enjoyed so much power, prestige, influence and praise as Nur Jahan.

Mehr-un-Nisa or Nur Jahan was the daughter of Ghiyas Beg, who belonged to a distinguished family of Persia, which had fallen upon bad days. Finding his life in Persia intolerable, he started for India with his wife and children, under the protection of a caravan led by a rich merchant named Malik Masud. With his kind help they travelled to Agra, the capital of Emperor Akbar. Later Ghiyaz Beg was appointed by Akbar into the imperial service and was later honoured with the title of Itimad-ud-Daulah. He rose steadily in rank and influence. By 1595 he held a mansab of 300 and the important office of Diwan of Kabul.[1]

The story of her romantic meeting with Jahangir who was greatly influenced by her beauty and wit, may or may not be true. But it would seem likely that Jahangir was deeply touched by her beauty grace and wisdom. At the age of seventeen she was married to Ali Quli Khan, entitled Sher Afghan Khan, whom Akbar had appointed as governor of Burdwan. In 1605, Jahangir ascended the throne of Hindustan. Sher Afghan was suspected of conspiring against the emperor. Jahangir authorised his foster brother Qutbuddin to send Sher Afghan to his court in case of disobedience Qutbuddin proceeded to Burdwan. As soon as Sher Afghan entered the camp of Qutbuddin he was surrounded by soldiers. Suspecting treachery, Sher Afghan drew his sword and struck Qutbuddin. The latter's followers however killed him.[2]

Jahangir had Sher Afghan's widow and daughter, Ladli Begam brought to the court. Later Jahangir married her in 1611.

The circumstances of the death of Sher Afghan and the emperors marriage with Nur Jahan, is a subject of great controversy among historians.

At the time of her marriage to Jahangir was about to complete his forty-second year, while Nur Jahan was thirty-four years of age. After her marriage she received successive titles of Nur Mahal (the light of the palace) and Nur Jahan (the light of the world). She would ride and hunt on horseback and would shoot with a steady hand. In 1613, she succeeded to the rank of Padishah Begam or first lady of the Realm.

Nur Jahan was endowed with a strong intellect and quick understanding she was highly educated and had a tremendous aesthetic sense. She was extremely fond of poetry, music and painting. She composed verses in Persian. Many verses composed by Nur Jahan were found in Khafi Khan's *Muntakhab-ul-Lubab* and Sujan Raya's *Khulasat-ul-Tawarikh.*

Nur Jahan was a passionate lover of books and she maintained a big personal library of her own. She enriched her library with rare and valuable works. She purchased for her library the Diwan of Mirza Kamran for three mohurs. On the first page of this Diwan these lines occur, "Three Muhars the price of this treasure, Nawab Nur-un-Nisa Begam". This shows that she had bought this book before her marriage with Jahangir.

She devised new dresses, ornaments and styles of fashion and decoration. She designed many new dresses of brocade lace and gown etc. Nur Mahali, (a complete set of garment for the bridegroom which cost Rs. 25 only). Dudami (flowered muslin), Panchtolia for Orhins (veils), Badlah (silver thread), Kinari (lace) and Farsh-i-Chandani (carpets of sandalwood colour) are famous among the dresses designed by the first lady of the realm. The costumes designed by her remained famous for many centuries. Writing a century later, Khafi Khan remarks that the fashions introduced by Nur Jahan still governed society and that the old ones survived only among the Afghans in backward towns.[3]

Nur Jahan had also equal love for ornaments. She herself designed many new gold ornaments. She laid down new patterns and elegant designs.

In fact, the fashion she introduced continued to govern the society till the reign of Aurangzeb. Nur Jahan also took interest in music. She was also a good singer.

Nur Jahan was a generous person. She had made it a rule to defray the expenses of the marriage of orphan girls and to distribute considerable charity everyday. For eleven years, she carried on the administration of the greatest empire in the world by her wise statesmanship and her great influence on the emperor was clearly visible when farmans were issued under her seal, and her name was struck on coins. Her father was promoted to the rank of prime minister, while his two sons also received responsible posts. She was elevated to the rank of Padshah Begam or the first lady of the realm.

The power enjoyed by her and her family members and prince Khurram made historians call this small but influential group as Nur Jahan Junta.

History and legend have surrounded her personality. She is reputed to have been the inventor of the altar of roses, though the credit really belongs to her mother. On once occasion she is said to have shot four tigers with gun and arrow, the emperor was so pleased with her skill that he presented her with a diamond ring. The story of how a stray arrow from her bow killed a washerman on the river bank near the royal palace, and how on a complaint from the washerman's wife. Jahangir ordered Nur Jahan to be brought to his court of justice like any ordinary criminal, is well known.

The last years of her married life was not very happy. Prince Khurram (Shah Jahan) Jahangir, eldest son and successor to the throne revolted. He was soon subdued by the help of a powerful amir, Mahabat Khan, governor of Kabul. The latter himself soon afterwards roused Nur Jahan's suspicions and was ordered to present himself before the emperor, who was then on his way to Kabul. Mahabat Khan had to obey the royal behest, but succeeded in capturing the emperor. With great difficulty Nur Jahan freed her husband. Jahangir however due to his failing health did not live long. He died on the way from Kashmir to Lahore in 1627. He was laid to rest in a garden at Lahore planted by Nur Jahan and his tomb at Shahdara a suburb of Lahore, is a fine, e.g. of Mughal architecture.

After the death of her husband, she lived a quiet and a solitary life. She lived to the advance age of seventy-two and died in 1646, nineteen years after her husband.

Nur Jahan exercised a healthy influence upon her husband. She looked after her husband with care and devotion. It was owing to her influence that he reduced his excessive drinking habit. She relieved him much of the drudgery of state administration, and successfully enhanced the splendour of the Mughal court and ably seconded the efforts of her husband in patronizing learning and arts. She extended her patronage to women.

Nur Jahan built a mosque at Srinagar. This mosque was known as Pathar Masjid, because it was built by *pathar* or stones. It was also called Shahee (royal) mosque. This mosque was built in 1623 A.D. She also built many Sarais. She is credited of building several gardens. She built a garden known as Shah-Dara near Lahore.

Nur Jahan was also well skilled in the art of hunting. Very often she accompanied her royal consort Jahangir in many of his hunting trips.

NOTES

1. Nath, Renuka, *Notable Mughal and Hindu Women in the 16th and 17th Centuries A.D.*, Inter-India Publications, New Delhi, 1990.
2. Prasad, Beni, *History of Jahangir*, Fifth Edition, The Indian Press (Publication) Pvt. Ltd., Allahabad, 1962.
3. Madhavananda, Swami, Majumdar, Ramesh Chandra, *Great Women of India*, Published by Swami Ananyananda, President, Advaita Ashrama, Mayavati Pithoragarh, Himalayas, Calcutta, 1982.

6

Mumtaz Mahal

(1593–1631)

The lady of the Taj Mumtaz Mahal was the beloved wife of the famous Mughal emperor Shahjahan. Her husband immortalised her name by erecting a great mausoleum over her tomb.

The original name of Mumtaz Mahal was Arjumand Banu Begam or Honourable lady. She was the granddaughter of Mirza Ghiyas Beg also styled as Itimad-ud-Daulah, daughter of Asaf Khan, and niece of the great Mughal empress Nurjahan. She was born in 1593 A.D. during the reign of Akbar.

Arjumand Bano Begam was betrothed to prince Khurram, when she was fourteen years old. The betrothal ceremony took place in the year 1607 A.D.

Mumtaz Mahal was also a remarkable in the field of learning. She was a talented and cultured lady. She was well-versed in Persian and could compose poems in that language. Mumtaz Mahal also patronized a number of poets, scholars and other talented persons. A noted Sanskrit poet Vansidhara Mishra was favourite of Queen Mumtaz Mahal.

She also liked music. Sometimes she herself sang to please her imperial consort. Her songs were especially liked by the emperor.

Mumtaz Mahal was a lady of charitable disposition. She was always ready to help needy persons. Everyday when the emperor came to Shah-Burj, Mumtaz Mahal presented before the emperor the case of needy persons. In this work she was assisted by Nazir Sati-un-Nissa. Sati-un-Nissa informed the empress about the poor and needy women. She also reported to the empress the case of unmarried poor girls. Mumtaz Mahal puts these cases before the emperor. The emperor spent a large sum of money for these needy persons. Some poor women received grants of land, some received stipends and some received in cash rupees. Suitable bridegrooms were selected for the unmarried girls and their marriages were celebrated from the imperial purse. Mumtaz Mahal's kindness and help gave many distressed people a new life.

Mumtaz Mahal died at Burhanpur. Her body was at first deposited temporarily in the Zainabad garden on the banks of river Tapti opposite Burhanpur. A temporary tomb was made there. After six months of her death on 1st December, 1631 A.D., her body was sent to Agra. A large tract of land was selected for the burial place at Agra. This land was on the banks of Jamuna and south of Agra city. The construction of the Taj Mahal was begun early in 1632 A.D. and was completed in January 1643 A.D. It was completed under the supervision of Mukarramat Khan and Mir Abdul Karim. It was constructed at an expense of 40 lakhs of rupees.[1]

During her life Mumtaz Mahal gained a lot of confidence of her husband and she became the keeper of his seal and access to all his farmans. On her request, the royal seal was entrusted to the father. Mumtaz Mahal was also known as Kudsia Begam and Nawab Alia Begam.

Mumtaz Mahal died at the age of thirty-nine years, four months and four days. She passed away in 1631.

NOTE

1. Nath, Renuka, *Notable Mughal and Hindu Women in the 16th and 17th Centuries A.D.*, Inter-India Publication, New Delhi, 1990.

7

Jahan Ara

(1613 — 1683)

Jahan Ara was the daughter of Mughal emperor Shah Jahan and his wife Mumtaz Mahal. She was born on 21st of Safar, 1023 A.H. (23rd March, 1614 A.D.), at Ajmer. Shah Jahan and Mumtaz Mahal took a keen interest in her education. A talented and educated lady Sati-un-Nisa was appointed her tutor. This lady at first taught Quran to Jahan Ara and after this Persian was taught. Lessons were also imparted in prose and poetry. Other subjects were also taught to her.

After the death of Jahangir, Shah Jahan ascended the throne. Shah Jahan conferred on her the title of "Padshah Begam" (The Empress of Princess). She also received a gift of one lakh of ashrafis and four lakh of rupees. Shahjahan fixed for her an annual allowance of six lakhs of rupees. Half of this annual allowance was paid to her in cash and jagirs were assigned to her for the other half.

This gifted princess had the unique distinction of being called Begam Sahib (the Begam par excellence). Jahan Ara was intellectually gifted and always worked for the welfare of the poor and the needy. Like her brother Dara Shikoh, she had a deep strain of mysticism in her character, and in her early life imbibed a passionate love for the Chishtiya Saints of India, specially Khwaja Muinuddin, to whose sanctuary at Ajmer she added a large and beautifully decorated hall. She wrote biographical accounts on the saints and his successors, which were collected under the title of Munis-al-Arwah (The Companion of the Souls), and became very popular. Shahabiya was another book of Jahan Ara. This was the biography of Mulla Shah who initiated the Qadiriyya order of Sufis.

Jahan Ara Begam was not only a learned lady, but she also promoted education. Learned people received rewards from her. Hasan Beg Rafi and Nazr Muhammad Khan received a reward of five hundred rupees from her for a poem in praise of the Bagh-i-Hayat Buksh garden. Like several other Mughal princesses, Jahan Ara remained unmarried. Her father's love for her and her filial devotion to him form indeed a remarkable chapter in Mughal history.[1]

When her brother (Aurangzeb) relationship with his father deteriorated, her sympathies were with Dara Shikoh, who was the eldest son. She tried her utmost to dissuade Aurangzeb from defying his father and ousting his elder brother from his rightful place. She however failed, Aurangzeb succeeded in occupying the throne and he in turn confined his father Shah Jahan in the Agra fort. Though he gave her the honorific title of Badshah Begam and a jagir (present of land) with an annual income of rupees seventeen lakhs, yet she completely cut herself off from court life and shared the confinement of her father with steadfast loyalty. Her father died in 1666 A.D., and she followed him sixteen years later at the age of seventy.

Like her father Jahan Ara was very fond of building edifices and laying beautiful gardens. The most remarkable among her buildings is the Jama Masjid of Agra. Another mosque, known as the mosque of Mulla Badakhshi, was built by her in Kashmir, while several gardens in Delhi and Agra owed their origin to her fine taste. For promotion of education she founded a madrasa which was attached to Jama Masjid at Agra. She designed the place of a bazar in Lahore which was built under her instruction. The bazar was known as Chowk Sarai.

After her death she left a property worth three crores of rupees, all of which she bequeathed to Khwaja Muinuddin's sanctuary, but Aurangzeb permitted only one crore to be spent according to her desire, since, he argued, legally a bequest could be made only upto one-third of one's property.

She was buried in a small tomb made of polished white marble with delicately carved lattice-work which she had built herself in the sanctuary of Hazrat Nizamuddin Auliya in Delhi.[2]

NOTES

1. Nath, Renuka, *Notable Mughal and Hindu Women in the 16th and 17th Centuries A.D.*, Inter-India Publication, New Delhi, 1990.
2. Madhavananda, Swami, Majumdar, Ramesh Chandra, *Great Women of India*, Published by Swami Ananyananda, President, Advaita Ashrama, Mayavati Pithoragarh, Himalayas, Calcutta, 1982.

8

Roshanara Begam

(1617—1671)

Roshanara Begam was the second surviving daughter of Shahjahan and Mumtaz Mahal. She was born on August 24, 1617 at Burhanpur. She was younger than Jahan Ara and Dara Shikoh and Shah Shuja and elder than Aurangzeb. She remained a spinster for her whole life like her elder sister Jahan Ara Begam. When Shahjahan became emperor, he fixed an annual allowance of one lakh rupees for her.

Roshnara Begam was a very staunch supporter of her younger brother Aurangzeb. When the war of succession broke out among the sons of Shahjahan, she fully supported the cause of Aurangzeb. She sent him all the gold and silver she could. Not only this she supplied valuable information to him.[1]

Roshanara Begam was an educated and a very talented lady. She was very good at the art of writing. She also possessed a good aesthetic sense. She built a garden at Delhi, to the west of Sabzi Mandi, the suburb of the vegetable market which was known as Roshanara Bagh. This garden was laid in 1650 A.D. by her. After her death, she was buried in her own garden-house, an elaborate white pavilion with creeper clad wall, standing on a low wide platform in the centre of the upper terrace in the garden still called by her name. Today the garden is not in its previous position but the tomb of Roshanara Begam is still in good order.

She passed away in the thirteenth year of the reign of Aurangzeb on September 11, 1671 A.D.

NOTE

1. Nath, Renuka, *Notable Mughal and Hindu Women in the 16th and 17th Centuries A.D.*, Inter-India Publication, New Delhi, 1990.

9

Zibunnisa

(1638—1702)

Zibunnisa was the gifted daughter of Aurangzeb. She was born on the 10th Shawwal, 1047 A.H. (February 15, 1638 A.D.). Her mother was Dilras Banu Begam who was a Persian and chief queen of Aurangzeb.

From her early childhood Zibunissa Begam showed her desire to study. She started her studies at a very tender age. Aurangzeb appointed for her a lady tutoress named Hafiza Maryam. This lady was well-versed in Arabic and Persian. Owing to her father's teaching, she became proficient in the knowledge of Quran. When she was only seven years old, she became Hafiz (one who knew the Quran by heart). Aurangzeb was extremely proud of his daughter and rewarded her with 30,000 gold coins. He also arranged a huge feast. Besides Hafiza Maryam, she was also tutored by some other best scholars of the time, famous among them was Mulla Said Ashraf Mazandrani. He cultivated a taste for poetry in her and she later became a poetess of distinction. Shah Rustam Ghazi, another tutor, directed her literary tastes. She also studied mathematics and astronomy.

She was a great scholar and contributed towards the advancement of literature in Urdu and Persian. She made rapid progress in her studies. She acquired great proficiency in the Arabic and Persian language and several important branches of learning. She gained considerable skill in calligraphy. She could write Nastaliq Naskh and Shikastah very perfectly. Her love for Persian poetry is well known, and she wrote elegant verses full of rare pathos under the pen-name of Makhfi (the concealed one). Her poems have been collected and have acquired wide celebrity under the title of *Diwan-i-Makhfi*.

She also started writing a commentary on the Quran but was stopped by her father. She also authored *Zib-ul-Tafsir* and *Zib-ul-Munshaat*.[1]

Several distinguished scholars of her time wrote and flourished under the patronage and dedicated their work to her. The poets among her circle were Nasir Ali Saib, Samsh Wali Ullah, Brahmin and Bahraaz. She had a large private library containing beautiful and richly illuminated copies of important literary works, and she spent most of her time in the quiet pursuit of knowledge. She took keen interest in music when she recited Quran, and moved her listeners to tears. She was also fond of playing Chausar. She also invented a woman garment known as Angya Kurti. This was a modified form of dress of the women of Turkestan. The modification was done to suit Indian condition. She was a kind-hearted lady and she always helped the needy person. She helped the widows and orphans. Not only this, every year she sent pilgrims to Mecca and Medina. She was a spinster. Zibunnisa never shared her father's orthodoxy. She was a sufi. She was imprisoned in the fort of Salimgarh in 1681 A.D. and spent the rest of her life there. She died in A.D. 1701-2, in the life time of her father. Her burial place has never been correctly located.

NOTE

1. Madhavananda, Swami, Majumdar, Ramesh Chandra, *Great Women of India*, Published by Swami Ananyananda, President, Advaita Ashrama, Mayavati Pithoragarh, Himalayas, Calcutta, 1982.

10

Zinat-un-Nissa

(1644 — 1721)

Zinat-un-Nissa Begam was the second daughter of Aurangzeb. Her mother was Dilras Banu, daughter of Shah Nawaz Khan. She was born on 1st Shabban 1053 A.H. When Shahjahan heard the news of her birth, he gave her name Zinat-un-Nissa.

Aurangzeb personally took interest in her education. She acquired high proficiency "in the knowledge of the doctrines and the necessary rules of the faith" under her father's supervision.

Zinat-un-Nissa remained a spinster throughout her life.

Zinat-un-Nissa also possessed poetic talent. She wrote her own epitapt, which runs this:

> "In my grave the grace of God is my only help. It is enough if the shadow of the cloud of mercy covers my tomb."[1]

Zinat-un-Nissa was very famous for her noble deeds. Supported by her bounty a large number of people received their livelihood.

Zinat-un-Nissa was a great architect. She built many caravan-sarais for the help of people. She also built a mosque in Delhi, known as Zinat-un-Masjid or the 'Ornament of Mosque'. It was also known as Kauri Masjid or Maidan Mosque. This was built in 1700 A.D.

Zinat-un-Nissa also built her tomb during her life time within the enclosures of the mosque. It was built of red sandstone.

Her tomb was demolished immediately after the revolt of 1857 A.D. The marble monument was removed and the grave was levelled with the ground. It was used as an artillery barrack after the revolt.

Zinat-un-Nissa looked after her father Aurangzeb's household in the Deccan. After the death of Aurangzeb, war of succession to the throne began between his sons Muhammad Muazzam Shah, Azam Shah and Kam Baksh. In this war of succession Zinat-un-Nissa took the side of Azam Shah and accompanied him in his march from the Deccan to Delhi. Though Azam Shah was killed by Muazzam Shah who afterward was known as Bahadur Shah, treated her well. He doubled her allowance and confered on her the title of "Padshah Begam". She enjoyed respect under the reign of Bahadur Shah's successor Jahangir Shah and Farrukhsiyar. She died on May 9, 1721 A.D.[2]

NOTES

1. Machicol Margaret (Ed.), *Poems by Indian Women*, Published by Association Press, Calcutta, 1923, pp. 36, 79.
2. Nath, Renuka, *Notable Mughal and Hindu Women in the 16th and 17th Centuries A.D.,* Inter-India Publications, New Delhi, 1990.

11

Qudsia Begam

(1801—1881)

Nawab Qudsia Begam was the daughter of Nawab Ghaus Mohammad Khan. She was also known as Nawab Gauhar Begam. She was born in 1801 and was better known as Qudsia III. Her reign marks the beginning of female rulers of Bhopal state.[1]

There is not much written record of her early education. A reliable historian of her age gives ample proof of her being well educated. Her education was mostly religious in nature. Major Heighes, who was an officer in the Bengal army, in his well researched book, *History of Bhopal* writes about Nawab Qudsia Begam in the following words:

> "Begam would have been 18 or 19 years then but she was really well educated and had an extremely sharp mind. This is why she was able to control the affairs of the state and do all that was required, of her own."[2]

At the age of fifteen she was married to Nawab Nazir-ud-Daulah Nazar Mohammed Khan. Nineteen months after her marriage she gave birth to a girl who later on was known as Nawab Sikander Begam. At a young age of seventeen she became a widow and the ruler of the state. She ruled the state as a regent and lived to assert a powerful influence on the history of the dominion till her death in 1881. Between the death of her husband Nazar Mohammed Khan and the marriage of her daughter to Jahangir Mohammed Khan, Qudsia Begam, exercised all the powers of the ruler as a regent and continued to do so even after her daughter's marriage.

She emerged from behind the veil, and became a strong ruler of the Bhopal state. Sultan Jahan Begam wrote that her grandmother believed that "ruling from behind the veil was like working in the dark."[3] She even took permission from her brothers, and the state officials who apparently gave her. In fact, her brothers quoted cases 'among ancient ruling families of women who had not only ruled but held durbars.'[4]

In the early years of her reign she wanted to demonstrate to her adversaries her power to run the administration. She displayed all her military skills, her ability to use weapons, and ride horse or elephants. She was indeed successful in convincing her contemporaries that she was right person to rule the state in the times of war, disorientation, and political instability.[5]

As a ruler of her state she lived a simple and austere life. Her great-granddaughter, Sultan Jahan Begam states that, "She came from a race of Afghan soldiers, who were simple men, who cared much more for a trusty sword and a stout-hearted horse than luxurious places."[6] Her simple and modest life is also reflected in the kind of clothes she wore. Sultan Jahan Begam depicts that........

> "Her dress consisted of the narrow Mahommedan trousers a long shirt to the knee, and a head dress after the Arabian fashion. At times the materials was sumptuous and at others quite simple, and in the latter years of her life she wore garments of quite coarse material and a head dress of ochre coloured long cloth. As far as the author remembers, she seldom if ever wore ornaments except on the 9th of the Zilhy month in honour of the day of the haj pilgrimage, but she soon took them off as they were irksome to her."[7]

She was a tolerant ruler who gave charitable grants to the Hindus and Muslims alike. In fact, her charitable endowments extended as far as Arabia. According to her account she spent Rs. 20,000 for the charitable and religious purposes. Her charitable character and her sense of welfare and justice caused Qudsiya to be regarded as the reincarnation of Mamola Bai by her Hindu subject.[8]

The British regarded Qudsiya Begam with a mixture of fascination and suspicion. Sir John Malcolm writes of her thus:

> "She is described as very young, being only seventeen, she is, besides, stated to be of a mild disposition, and to have been strongly attached to the Nabob, who treated her with unusual consideration ...."[9]

It is significant to note that Nawab Qudsiya Begam tried to disprove of the above opinion that was held by the British. She was unveiled when she appeared in the public and was noticed with astonishment. Her activities in the field of sports and her military skills caused even more astonishment. She was said to ride horses, as well as camels and elephants taking full part in hunting and marital activities.

Some of the significant reforms that were undertaken by her are as follows:

Contribution made towards the construction of railways—Nawab Qudsiya Begam contributed greatly towards the construction of railways in her state. In 1868, she contributed 15 lakh rupees for its construction. She made this contribution in instalments of two lakh rupees per annum. Another significant construction work that was undertaken by her was laying the foundation of Bhopal water works and pipelines throughout the state. These were completely financed from her Privy Purse. She paid nearly six lakh of rupees to erect a pumping station. The work was carried out by a Scottish Engineer named David Cook.[10]

Some of the significant architectural works that was carried out during her reign was the construction of one of the greatest monuments of Bhopal a huge Friday Mosque. Its construction began in 1835, and was completed in 1857. It was supervised by some prominent architects.[11]

Qudsiya Begam financed the construction of the entire building which is said to have costed Rs. 565,000, 2 annas and 9 pice. She even attached a munificent religious endowment (*Waqf*) to it.[12]

During her rule religious activities gained public significance. The maulid (celebration of birth) of Abd-al-Qadir-al-Jilani (1088-1166), the founder of the Qadiriyya Sufi Order, was lavishly celebrated under her patronage.[13]

Throughout her life Qudsia Begam was renowned for her liberty, kindness of heart, and the simplicity of her life. She was greatly revered by all the people of Bhopal. The following account of her was given by William Kincard, Political Agent, during a Durbar held by him :

> "Throughout the Bhopal state she is remembered with love and reverence for many generous deeds of charity. Those deeds and alms to the poor and needy were done for the sake of God and not from the desire of fame, and I will abstain from describing all of them at this gathering as those present are fully aware of them. My audience, do you not offer your prayers in the great mosque which was built at the expenditure of great sums by her? Do you not know how many poor and needy persons are enabled to perform the pilgrimage to Mecca and Medina through grants of money made by the Begam, and thus fulfil a duty laid upon them by God which even many persons of moderate means are not able to perform."[14]

At Lord Lytton's great Durbar at Delhi in 1876, when Queen Victoria was proclaimed Empress of India, Qudsia Begam was granted the order of the Crown of India, and the grant was made known to her in an official letter which was brought to Bhopal by Colonel William Kincard, Political Agent. He held a Durbar and made the following speech :

> "I have much pleasure and happiness in making over the distinguished title and insignia of the Crown of India to the Nawab Begam Qudsia Sahiba which the Honourable Governor General has sent as a token of Her Imperial Majesty's regard for her loyalty and honour."[15]

During her reign she travelled widely. She visited the holy city of Benaras, Lucknow, Faizabad, Agra and other cities. In November 1863, she started on a pilgrimage to Mecca.

Qudsia Begam died in 1881 at the ripe age of eighty-one years. She was buried in the garden of her husband Aishbagh under an extremely unostentatious dome.

NOTES

1. Nawab Sultan Jahan Begam (tr. W.S. Davis), *Hayat-I-Qudsi: Life of the Nawab Gauhar Begam Alias the Nawab Begam Qudsia of Bhopal*, London: Kegan Paul, Trench, Trubner & Co. Ltd., New York: E.P. Dulton & Co., 1918.
2. *Begamat-e-Bhopal*, p. 36.
3. Shah Jahan Begam, *Taj-ul-ikbal: Tarikh Bhopal*, or *The History of Bhopal*, Translated H.C. Barstow, Calcutta, 1876.
4. .... She was now 34 years old and she first consulted her brother Mian Muiz Mohammed Khan and Mian Faujdar Mohammed Khan and asked them whether they had prejudices against her relinquishing the Purdah like the ignorant people. Both brothers agreed with her view and quoted cases among ancient ruling families of women who had not only ruled but had held Darbars. They promised to support her if Nawab Jahangir Mohammed Khan and his father and brother raised difficulties, and after consulting the officers of state she gradually forsook the Purdah. For details see Nawab Sultan Jahan Begam, *Hayat-I-Qudsi: Life of the Nawab Gauhar Begam Alias Nawab Begam Qudsia* (tr. by. W.S. Davis), London: Kegan Paul, Trench, Trubner & Co. Ltd., New York: E.P. Dulton & Co. 1918, p. 105.
5. Preckel, Claudia, *Begums of Bhopal*, Lotus Collection, Roli Books, New Delhi, 2000, p. 32.
6. Sultan Jahan Begam, *op. cit.*, p. 150.
7. *Ibid.*, p. 151.
8. Preckel, Claudia, *op. cit.*, p. 38. See also Mittal, Kamla, *History of Bhopal State: Development of Constitutional, Administration and National Awakening 1901-1949*, Munshiram Manoharlal Publishers Pvt. Ltd., New Delhi, 1990, p. 21.
9. Sultan Jahan Begam, *op. cit.*, p. 24.
10. Preckel, Claudia, *op. cit.*, p. 37.

    Mittal, Kamla, *op. cit.*, pp. 20-21.
11. *Ibid.*
12. Preckel, Claudia, *op. cit.*, pp. 37-38.
13. *Ibid.*
14. Ashfaq, Sayed Ali, *Bhopal—Past and Present: A Brief History of Bhopal and Madhya Pradesh from Hoary Past upto the Present*, Time, 3rd ed., Bhopal, 1986, p. 144.
15. Sultan Jahan Begam, *op. cit.*, p. 144.

12

Nawab Sikander Begam

(1819—1868)

Nawab Sikander Begam was the second in the line of female lineage ruler of Bhopal. She was the daughter of Qudsia Begam and Nawab Nazar Mohammed Khan. She was extremely fortunate because on her birth there was great celebration for nearly seven days. Unfortunately she lost her father in her infancy and was brought up in the loving care of her mother.[1]

The initial education of Nawab Sikander Begam was supervised by her mother. For each subject that she had learnt, she had a separate teacher. All the teachers were well trained and saw to it that she understood each and every subject. In religious education she was first taught Quran. Later she was taught the explanation of it. She had mastered the Quran so well that she often quoted Quranic verses in her speeches and writings. She was also taught calligraphy and had a good knowledge of Persian language. In fact, in her official orders and rules she normally used this language. She learned horse riding, shooting, use of arrow and was good at javelin throwing. In fact, her training was so perfect that at a young and formative age she became an expert in the art of warfare.[2]

By the time Nawab Sikander Begam got married she had already completed her education. She was engaged to Nawab Jahangir Mohammed Khan and was finally married to him on April 18, 1835. Later her husband Nawab Jahangir Mohammed Khan was duly invested with the authority of the State on November 17, 1837. The relation between Nawab Sikander Begam and her husband was not coordial. The main difference that arose between husband and wife was over the questions of purdah. In April 1838, the Nawab inflicted a sword wound on Sikander's hand. It needed four stitches. It was reported that Nawab was unhappy because Sikander Begam appeared in public without purdah. The strained relation with her husband compelled her to leave him. She withdrew to the fort of Islamnagar accompanied by her mother Qudsia Begam. It was at this fort that she gave birth to her daughter Shah Jahan Begam on 29th July 1838. She was to be the future ruler of Bhopal. In 1844 her husband, Nawab Jahangir Mohammed Khan died. The questions of succession to the throne arose. Since Bhopal was a Princely State, having a British regent who had a great say in matters of succession, therefore on the death of the Nawab, the British Government recognized the succession of her daughter Shah Jahan Begam. She was proclaimed the Chief of the State, in the regency of her mother and maternal uncle Mian Faujdar Mohammed Khan. But soon this dual regency proved unsuccessful. Later Mian Faujdar Mohammed Khan had to resign and the entire administration of the State was left to Nawab Sikander Begam till her daughter came of the right age.

After her investiture as a Ruler of State, Sikander Begam worked day and night to undertake reforms in her state. Within six years of her regime she had paid off the total debt amounting to Rs. 23 lakhs, out of which Rs. 2,87,544 was paid off within first three years, and the rest by 1853. She later divided the whole State of Bhopal into three districts and 24 tehsils, so that it could be administered well. Each district was supervised by a Nazim (divisional officer). All the district headquarters were at an equal distance of 24 miles from Bhopal. The Nazims were mainly responsible for the supervision of the administration of criminal justice. They had to control the work of tehsildars.

Nawab Sikander Begam was genuinely interested in improving the lot of the cultivators. She is reported to have said :

> "The cultivators of the soil are our wealth; that we are able to rule and to live in the state in luxury, is owing to the labour and industry of these poor people."[3]

Civil Administration

Under her rule the condition of the inhabitants of the city of Bhopal had improved. Each new administrative unit was connected to the capital by newly designed roads. Roads were also constructed in every part of the city. Lamp-posts were set up on both the sides of the street and hundred of permanent houses were built. Shah Jahan Begam in her Account mentions that, "The people began to dress in respectable clothes, to eat good dinners, and also to live in good houses. The better class of inhabitants busied themselves in acquiring articles of culture and luxury."[4]

Police Reforms

The police department of the state was highly centralized and was put under the supervision of Thanedar. His salary was fixed and they were given a small piece of land directly from the State for cultivation.

Army Reform

Under the reign of Nawab Sikander Begam the Bhopal army was reformed. Her Highness spent Rs. 2 lakhs per annum to modernize the Bhopal contingent. She modernized the equipments they used, barracks were built for the troops, weekly inspection of all weapons was made compulsory, and the soldiers training was improved by sending them to Sehore for instruction in the modern art of war.

In 1857, the great uprising took place at Meerut and gradually spread throughout the country. Sikander Begam stood loyal to the British.

On the re-establishment of the British authority, the loyal services of Sikander Begam received appreciation from the British Government. It is significant to note that not a single European was killed in the great uprising. Even the British officers acknowledged this fact that no chief in the length and breadth of India proved a more staunch ally than the ruler of Bhopal. On the restoration of order in Bhopal state, Sikander Begam asked her claim to be regarded not as Regent, but as the Ruling Chief of Bhopal, on the strength of her services during the Mutiny, and also on the grounds that the recognition of her late husband Jahangir as Nawab was technically wrong, she in the same way as her daughter Shah Jahan being in fact the legitimate ruler, Shah Jahan Begam, who had come of age on 20th July, 1858, and was entitled to be invested with administrative powers, herself came forward and consented to the investiture of her mother as chief waiving all claims to the masnad during her lifetime. The British Government acceded to this and on 3rd March, 1860 Sikander Begam was formally installed as the Chief of Bhopal by the British Agent to the Governor-General Hamilton.

On 7th January, 1861 a durbar was arranged by Viceroy Canning at Jabalpur in which Sikander Begam was especially invited. The Begam was presented with a sanad conferring to her the pargana of Berasia which was under the Dhar State as a reward for her loyal services rendered during the uprising. In November of the same year Nawab Sikander Begam was invested with the G.C.S.I. at Allahabad. In this particular Durbar, the Begam was invested with the Most Exalted Order of the Star of India. In the same Durbar medals and titles were also conferred upon Maharaja Kyaji Rao Sindhia, the Nawab Sahib of Rampur and the Maharaja of Patiala.[5]

After being formally installed as the ruler of Bhopal, Nawab Sikander Begam continued her administrative reforms in Bhopal which is mentioned below.

Judiciary

The judiciary was remodelled and the laws were codified, various courts of law were established throughout Bhopal where civil and criminal cases were judged. The highest court of appeal was the Royal Court. The only exception to this was their jurisdiction over the British subject. She separated Hindu and Muslim laws. She was also responsible for the legislation of certain new laws which were published under the title Dustur-al-Amal Nizami (Instruction of Law and Order) in 1867. The laws were compiled according to those in British India unfortunately these instructions are no longer available.[6]

Educational Reforms

Nawab Sikander Begam was keenly interested in undertaking educational reforms in her state. She established Madrasa-i-Sulaymaniya.[7] This institution was named after her late grand-daughter Sulayman Jahan Begam. The curriculum of this institution emphasised on the teaching of Mathematics, Nagri, Urdu, Persian, Arabic and English. It is significant to note that even though Nawab Sikander Begam encouraged oriental languages and made Urdu the official language of Bhopal she saw to it that her daughter Shah Jahan Begam and her granddaughter Sultan Jahan Begam received private lessons in English. She realised that only a command of English, plus other abilities like arithmetics, could secure her own as well as her descendants position in the elite society.

She also established new Urdu and Hindi schools in each pargana of the State to promote the general education of her subject, both Muslims and Hindus. The local officers were instructed to encourage the people to send their children to schools. The teachers in these schools were suitably renumerated.[8]

The second school that was established by the Begam was the Victoria School. Most of the teachers in this school were Anglo-Indians, and its director was a woman named Zabun-al-Nisa. Gold and silver lace-making, gold and silver embroidery, and many kinds of typical Indian needlework were taught to the students. Sikander Begam inspected this school once a week.[9]

In order to promote education in her state, the Begam spent rupees one million to establish new schools including books and other educational materials.

Her efforts bore fruits. The number of pupils both Hindus and Muslims increased rapidly. In 1865, the Political Agent reported on the State of Education in Bhopal. "The situation was most satisfactory". About 12 to 15 per cent of the population could read and write whereas, for example, the neighbouring State of Narsingarh had no school at all, and other states had only one school. Nearly 48 schools had existed in the Bhopal State in 1872.[10]

Sikander Begam herself was a reputed scholar. She wrote an account of her pilgrimage to Mecca in 1864, titled *Safar-nama Hijaz* (The Account of the Travel to the *Hijaz*). This was translated into English and was handed to the British representatives. She also wrote on the history and administration during her reign. Some of her well known works on the above theme are—*Tuzuk-i-Sikanderi* and *Ain-i-Sikander*. They are composed in prose. She also depicted her ideas in verse. Her diwan (collection of poems) titled *Diwan-i-Shirin* contains many fine ghazals. Some of the Europeans called her "a woman of fine Elizabethan taste" because of her literary abilities. All her books were printed in the *Matba'a-i-Sikandari* (Sikander Printing Office) which was founded by the ruler for disseminating her work.[11] It is significant to note that during the reign of Nawab Sikander Begam the first Census was taken during her last days. The population of Bhopal as reflected in the Report was 744,542. The second Census was conducted in the fourth year of Nawab Shah Jahan Begam's reign.

Medical Work

Nawab Sikander Begam wanted to improve the health status of her people. She introduced western system of medicine. The first small allopathic hospital was established in Bhopal in 1861.

In fact, by the end of her reign, Nawab Sikander Begam had transformed the State of Bhopal from an Afghan warrior principality into a modern, centralized state along Islamic lines.

Nawab Sultan Jahan Begam was full of praise of the reforms that was undertaken by her grandmother. In her account she mentions that :

> "Nawab Sikander Begam holds the same place in the history of Bhopal that Emperor Akbar holds in the history of India."[12]

An interesting view of the Begam is given by Major Charles Macpherson, the Political Agent, who writes in 1854, notes that all the three Begams of Bhopal were without purdah—Qudsia, Sikander and Shah Jahan Begam. The last of whom was sixteen years of age.

"The grandmother and mother ride, spear and shoot grandly or have been used to do so .... The Regent is a wonderful woman in the way of government. She talks exactly in her way like the fastest European woman you may happen to know, for example mixing politics with her personalities. I happen to say somewhat emphatically that everything depended on the way a system was worked, on the 'amal' (enterprise) that everything in fact was 'amal' and wished you had seen how she turned to her two ministers (Jamiluddin Khan and Lala Kishen Ram) sitting dumb some way off, and cried 'Gentlemen, do you hear, that is for you, 'amal' is everything."[13]

Nawab Sikander Begam was a devout Muslim. She undertook pilgrimage to Mecca and wrote about her experience there. This is vividly portrayed in her book *Safar-nama Hijaz*. She built the beautiful Moti Masjid (Pearl Mosque). This mosque is patterned on the Jam'a Mosque (Friday Mosque) of Delhi.

During her reign many eminent scholars came to Bhopal. The most prominent among them was Jamal-ad-Din. He was later appointed as Wazir or Prime Minister. Scholars were also invited from Yemen. Two significant scholars whose names are mentioned in the records are—Zayn-al-Abidin, Ibn Muhsin-al-Hudaydi, and his brother Husain Ibn Muhsin. While Husain worked as a teacher in one of the local Madrasa, his brother Zayn-al-Abidin was appointed as the state quazi.

Scholars and poets also came to Bhopal from Delhi, Lucknow and Caunpore (now Kanpur). The activities of the scholars enriched the cultural heritage of Bhopal State. The languages that developed in Bhopal city were—Arabic, Persian, Urdu and the English language.

Thus, under the able rule of Nawab Sikander Begam there was all-round progress and development in the state of Bhopal.

She died on 20th October, 1868 at the age of fifty-one years. She was buried in the Farhat Afza Garden which she herself had laid out. Although born to rank and grandeur, she loved simplicity, always so averse from all the forms of outward display of wealth that she even forbade the erection of a dome over her grave.

NOTES

1. *Begamat-e-Bhopal,* p. 45.
2. Preckel Claudia, *op. cit.*, pp. 48-49.
3. Sultan Jahan Begam, *An Account of My Life: Gohur-i-Ikbal,* Vol. II..............., Trans. C.H. Payne, London: Murray, 1912, p. 10.
4. Shah Jahan Begam, Taj-Ul-Ikbal, p. 224.
5. Nawab Sultan Jahan Begam, *op. cit.*, p. 11.
6. Preckel, Claudia, *op. cit.*, pp. 65-66.
7. "For the peculiar demands of the Jagirdars, a special school was opened and she personally induced the younger generation of her relatives, and the sons of Jagirdars to join the school. Nawab Sikander Begam had established the 'Madrasa-i-Sulaimania', in memory of Nawab Sulayman Jahan Begam. My mother greatly improved the school by creating separate classes for teaching Arabic, Persian, Urdu and Hindi, and classes were opened to give instruction in the English language also. Her Highness presented an excellent library to this institution. Education in English was gradually encouraged, until the school rose to the status of a High School, and was finally affiliated to the University of Calcutta, in 1892.

   For details see, Nawab Shahjahan, *op. cit.*, p. 193, Nawab Sultan Jahan Begam, Hayat-i-Shahjehani, p. 86.
8. Preckel, Claudia, *op. cit.*, p. 67.
9. Nawab Sultan Jahan Begam, *op. cit.*, p. 88, see also Preckel, Claudia, *op. cit.*, p. 67.
10. Preckel, Claudia, *op. cit.*, pp. 68-69.
11. *Ibid*, 71. See also, Mittal Kamla, *op. cit.*, pp. 26-27.
12. Nawab Sultan Jahan Begam, *An Account of My Life: Gohur-I-Ikbal*, p. 5.
13. Bhopal State Gazetteer, Vol. III, pp. 30-31.

13

Nawab Faizunnessa Chaudhurani

(1834—1903)

Nawab Faizunnessa Chaudhurani was born in an aristocratic zamindar family of Bengal. She had a very happy and memorable childhood. Both studies and play were given due importance by her parents. She spent her childhood behind strict purdah and was educated at home. Though her family spoke in Urdu like most Sharif families did, Faizunnessa through her own quest for education and love of knowledge acquired mastery over Bengali, Sanskrit, Urdu and Persian.

Faizunnessa having lived in the post-1857 period was effected by the social reformist activities which had engulfed most of the presidencies. She was of the view that for any amount of progress, especially of Muslim society, modern education and womens education in particular was the only answer. It is interesting to note that when liberal reformers like, Sir Syed Ahmed Khan and Abdul Lateef did not see the need for promoting women's education beyond the rudimentary stage, she foresaw the importance of both Muslim men and women acquiring western education. To translate her views on education into practice she established a free Madrasa at her residence in Paschimgaon in Comilla which today functions as Faizunnessa Degree College. This initial success motivated her further to established in 1901 an English middle school named after her daughter, Badrunnessa. She also set up primary schools at each of her administrative centres (*kacharis*) in her estate. Perhaps one of her single greatest achievement was the establishment of an English medium school for girls in 1873. The Faizunnessa Girls'

Pilot High School was designed for pardanashin girls. She was assisted in her endeavour by Kalicharan De, the famous Brahmo leader of Comilla. A hostel was subsequently added to the school. Many women who later became eminent in different fields studied in this school. It was later taken up by the government and converted into a high school.[1]

Thus, the contribution of Faizunnessa in promoting women's education in Bengal made her the pioneer. In 1889, she received the title of Nawab from Queen Victoria for the administration of her estate and her philanthropic activities. Douglas, the Magistrate of Comilla, impressed by Faizunnessa, recommended her to the Queen for a title.

The award of the title Nawab to a Muslim lady in those times created quite a stir and was flashed in contemporary newspapers.

Faizunnessa was a prolific writer. She wrote a book entitled, *Rupjalal.* This was her only extant literary work, which was published from Dhaka in 1876. Rupjalal is a remarkable hybrid picture of an age in transition, of a sensibility poised between the medieval punthi mentality and the modern prose one. Most scholars refer to it as a long poem. The greater part of the book is written in a sing song style; this is interspersed by passages written in chaste prose reminiscent of Bankimchandra Chatterjee. The book revolves around the romantic yearning of Prince Jalal for Princess Rupbano. The book is considered semi-autobiographical. Its tone and temper differs distinctly from the literary traditions of the future *bhadramahilas* who were deeply influenced by the writings of Bankimchandra Chatterjee, Sarat Chandra Chatterjee, Tagore, Mir and other modern writers, would not have allowed themselves the frankly sexual imagery and allusions in Rupjalal.

In this book she added a short autobiographical note. She mentions in her autobiography that on reaching adolescence she married Mahamud Ghazi Chaudhuri who was distantly related to her. Faizunnessa describes the first few years of her marriage as being happy and her husband as being extremely devoted. She believed that, subsequently, her husband's first wife used black magic to win back Mahamud Ghazi's heart and to make him hate her. She resolved never to return to her husband. She returned to her parental home to assume responsibility of the estates and devoted her life to philanthrophy, social work piety and study. She was an efficient administrator, though her public dealings were always conducted behind a curtain, observing purdah in its strictest and literal sense.[2]

NOTES

1. Ray, Bharati, (Ed), *From the Seams of History: Essays on Indian Women*, Oxford University Press, New Delhi, 1995.
2. Minault, Gail, *Secluded Scholars: Women's Education and Muslim Social Reform in Colonial India*, Oxford University Press, New Delhi, 1998.

14

Nawab Shah Jahan Begam

(1838—1901)

Nawab Shah Jahan Begam was the third female ruler of Bhopal. She succeeded as a ruler nominally on 11th April, 1845 after her father's death but after the death of her mother Nawab Sikander Jahan Begam, on 16th November 1868 she became the full-fledged ruler of the Bhopal state. Her daughter Sultan Jahan Begam who had been born on July 9th, 1858 was declared heir apparent.[1]

Nawab Shah Jahan Begam was tutored well by her mother. She also appointed some nobles to teach her daughter, the art of administration and politics, other than horse riding and shooting.[2] She received good education in her formative years. This contained some instruction in Persian, Urdu, as well as arithmetic, music and poetry. She had finished reading the Quran very early in life. In "Account of My Life", Sultan Jahan Begam states that Shah Jahan Begam had also inherited Sikander Begam's practical turn of mind. Besides instruction in the subject mentioned above, Shah Jahan Begam had received a full education in domestic economy and a thorough training in household duties. The Begam was used to doing needle work, dusting and cleaning, and arranging the various aspects of her household. She was able to cook her own food. According to Sultan Jahan Begam, her mother always had a number of girls around her in the palace with the object of teaching them embroidery. Besides this, she rewarded them with presents and gave money to them. She even presented their work to the Indian Princes and British officials as gifts.

She was an enlightened ruler and did not observe purdah (symbol of segregation). In fact on the death of her husband she came out of purdah.

This facilitated her to conduct the administration of her state. After the death of her first husband Nawab Baki Mohammed Khan she married again Maulvi Syed Siddiq Hasan Khan.

During her 32 years of reign she made many significant administrative reforms in her state. Some of the well known reforms were as follows.

Construction of Railways

To modernize the means of communication in Bhopal Nawab Shah Jahan Begam took much interest in the construction of Bhopal Railway. Regarding it Col. H. Daly in his memoirs of General Sir Henry Dermot Daly describes, "In the state of Central India of 1868 there was an entire lack of railway communication".[3] Further during an interview with Sir Henry Daly, who came to Bhopal during the reign of Nawab Shah Jahan Begam, she expressed the desire about the need for constructing railways in her state. She had final talk about the construction of state Railways with Daly that was to be constructed from Itarsi to Bhopal. It is significant to note that Nawab Shah Jahan Begam expressed the desire to construct it from the state treasury. She also persuaded her grandmother Qudsia Begam to advance money from her private purse. Thus, it was decided that a sum of 35 lakh rupees would be guaranteed of which 25 lakhs would be the contribution of the State in an annual instalments of five lakhs each, and 10 lakhs by Qudsia Begam in instalment of two lakh each and the whole amount to be advanced free of interest.[4] The Nawab also foresaw that a branch line connecting her capital with Itarsi would be of no advantage unless it could be continued beyond Bhopal to join Gwalior State railway at Ujjain or to be carried on through Bhilsa to Gwalior, thus opening up direct communication with Agra and the north of India. For this purpose the State and Qudsia Begam agreed to advance 50 lakh rupees of the state instead of 35 lakh rupees as previously decided.[5]

As a result of her efforts the opening ceremony of Bhopal railways took place on 18 November, 1884. In January 1897 another

Bhopal State railway was inaugurated. The opening ceremony was performed by the Hon'ble Col. Barr, Agent to the Governor-General of Central India. The total cost of the section of the line lying within the Bhopal territory was 18,89,068 rupees.

Coinage

In the reign of Nawab Shah Jahan Begam, in 1897, the state was introduced with the British coinage. Earlier to this, the state had minted its own silver and copper money, which was stamped with the name of the ruler and the date of issue.

Education and Literature

Nawab Shah Jahan Begam was a great scholar of repute. Some of her well known work that have been documented are—*Taj-ul-Iqbal* or the History of Bhopal, *Diwan-i-Shirin, Khazim-Atjal-Loghat*, *Tahzibun-Niswan* and *Loghat Shahjahan*.[7] She also compiled a Dictionary in the following six languages—Urdu, English, Persian, Arabic, Sanskrit and Turkish which she called as *Khazinat-ul-lugat*, or "Treasury of Languages". She was even prepared to distribute it to all important educational institutions throughout India.

The places where the dictionary was despatched is given below:

Places where the Dictionary was Despatched

Principal, Muir Central College	—	Allahabad
Principal, General Assembly's Institution, Calcutta	—	Calcutta
Principal, Presidency College	—	Calcutta
Principal, St. Stephens College	—	Delhi
Free Church	—	Calcutta
Inspector General of Education	—	C.P. Nagpur

Twelve copies were forwarded to the Director of Public Instruction in India.

Presidency College	—	Madras
Elphinstone College	—	Bombay
Madras Christian College	—	Madras
Agra College	—	Agra
Government College	—	Benaras
Canning College	—	Lucknow
Bareilly College	—	Bareilly
Mahomedan Anglo Oriental College	—	Aligarh
Oriental College	—	Lahore
Delhi College	—	Delhi
Government College	—	Jabalpore[9]

Her Court was often frequently visited by men of learning from all parts of India. Like her mother she was a great patron of learning. At the Madrasa-i-Sulaymaniya, which was founded by her mother Sikander Begam she added some new subjects to the curriculum and spent great money on furnishing it with latest equipments. Due to her sincere efforts the madrasa reached the level of a High School, and was later affiliated to the University of Calcutta in 1892. She also spent enormous sum of money on the foundation of new schools. Some thirty new schools were established by her, the most significant ones that were established by her were Madrasa-i-Bilquisiya.[10] This institution was meant for the orphan and destitute. It was named after Her Highness late granddaughter, Bilquis Jahan Begam.[11] The Prince of Wales School, was also meant for the orphans. This school was a technical school in which several handicrafts were taught. The curriculum emphasised on acquainting students with certain skills so that they would make a living for themselves. Some of the skills that was imparted to the students were—carpet making, tent making, knitting, lace work and silver and gold electroplating. This institution was solely meant for the boys, who received a monthly payment for their work, and also food and clothing at the expense of the state.[12] Two other school existed in the state of Bhopal, namely the Madrasa-i-Shah Jahangiriya for the teaching of oriental languages, and the Arabic School, founded by Jamal-ad-Din Khan. After the latters death in 1882, this school had nearly closed down, but Shah Jahan Begam came to its rescue.[13]

Art and Architecture

Like the Mughal Emperor Shah Jahan, Nawab Shah Jahan Begam beautified Bhopal by constructing important buildings. Some of which were the renowned for its design, and the quality of construction. She had three palaces constructed in the Mughal style for her personal use. They were the Ali Manzil, Benazir Palace and the Taj Mahal Palace. The Taj Mahal Palace was the most splendid of the three :

> "The frescoed gateways of the Taj Mahal Palace are so wide and spacious that a four-in-hand could be easily driven about within its portico .... There are hundreds of rooms in the palace. Every room was differently coloured and artistically furnished in colours to match. The carpets, chandeliers, chairs and sofas, the divans together with their covering, even the punkhas and the curtains were of the same colour as the ceiling and the walls of their respective rooms."[14]

The other significant building that was constructed in her reign was the Taj-al-Masjid. This literally means the 'Crown of Mosques' and was the second largest mosque of Asia. The area covered by the mosque is 248 by 94 feet, the height of the minarets is 206 feet, and the number of columns is 12. The crystal slabs, designed for its floor were prepared in England at a cost of seven lakh rupees. Over sixteen lakh of rupees were spent on its construction. The construction of this mosque could not be completed during the reign of Shah Jahan Begam. About the mosque, one of the court poet Dhulfiqar Ahmad writes the following lines :

"Oh God! Which building is more beautiful than this house.
And which strongly perfumed house is more worthy!
The lamps in which you can see the flames of the sky.
Are lights which blind the observer.
The house precious stones, which the eye has not seen. Not the ear heard throughout the centuries."[15]

The Taj-al-Masjid is built along the pattern of the Jama Masjid in Delhi which was built by the great Mughal Emperor, Shah Jahan.

Religious Reforms

Like her mother, Sikander Begam, Shah Jahan Begam wanted to win the support of orthodox Muslims for her reign by patronising Islamic scholarship at her court. For this reason she encouraged and supported scholars who wanted to study in Mecca and Medina. She also spent huge amount of money on those pilgrims who wanted to visit the above holy place.

In her Taj-ul-Ikbal, Shah Jahan Begam mentions various scholars who were invited to Bhopal during her reign. Muslim men of scientific attainments, maulvis, and hakims were attracted to Bhopal. Sa'd Ibn Hamd Ibn Atiq came to Bhopal from the Najd, because his father, Hamd Ibn Atiq, supported Siddiq Hasan Khan's ideas of reform; so did Muhammad Bashir as-Sahsawani who like the Nawab, was a member of the Ahl-i-hadith. Qazi Abd-al-Qayyum at Burhanawi, author of an Encyclopaedia, various doctors such as Asghar Husain Farrukhabadi, and other scholars were invited to Bhopal to become employees of the State. Shah Jahan Begam create a new class of elite, which were loyal to her. In *Taj-ul-Ikbal,* Shah Jahan Begam writes that some officials of high rank were loyal and efficient. These were the First Minister Jamal-ad-Din Khan, the First Minister's Secretary, as well as Diwan Thakur Pershad, Superintendent of the Ruler's office. The latter had great knowledge of finance and accounts Shah Jahan Begam underlined the essential qualification for a person to hold high place in the administration. In her account she states that :

> "During my reign, men of learning and capacity, good character, fidelity, honesty .... are respected and honoured as they deserve it."[16]

Welfare Measures

Nawab Shah Jahan Begam was a generous ruler. Her generosity to the needy and the deserving became well known not only in Bhopal but throughout India. Even Sultan Jahan Begam admits that:

> "In all other respects, the reign of Nawab Shah Jahan was a period of continued progress—a progress testifying to the hand of an enlightened and far-seeing ruler. But my mother was not only enlightened in a manner rarely to be met with amongst Mussalman ladies in India, she was, at the same time, generous, charitable, gentle in disposition, refined in manner, and faithful to her words .... During the famine of 1899, hundreds of human beings owed their lives to her liberality, and even strangers, who sought refuge in the state during the terrible time, were fed and cared for. She established a special fund for the relief of the poor, from which hundreds of people, daily, received money sufficient for their subsistence."[17]

Two new departments were established by her—namely Sadarabat and Masarif. The former was intended for the Hindu population and it offered them free rations daily. In addition, money for travelling was paid to them, along with their food expenses. The Masarif, gave grants and allowances to the Muslim widows, old persons and other people who were not able to earn their livelihood.

The greatest service that Shah Jahan Begam did was to open on hospital exclusively for the purdah women. In 1891, when His Excellency Lord Lansdowne visited Bhopal Shah Jahan Begam founded a hospital for women, taking care to add a class for the training of midwives. A qualified European lady doctor was placed incharge of it. Its opening ceremony took place on May 26th, 1892, on the occasion of the anniversary of Queen Victoria's accession to the throne.[18]

For women, she also built a new Pucca Inn near the Railway Station. She named it 'Sarai Sikanderi' in the memory of her mother. A special feature of the 'Sarai' was that travellers of all ages could find a suitable accommodation.

Though Shah Jahan Begam was a pious Muslim ruler, she was extremely tolerant towards other religions. She had many Hindu and Christian ministers. During her reign the most important lady at the Court was Madame Elizabeth de Bourbon, being the most important lady at Court. Further, she did not put any embargo to missionary activity in Bhopal. The earlier missionary activity concentrate on working at the leper asylum.

The various reforms that were undertaken by Nawab Shah Jahan Begam were fully appreciated by the British Government. As a consequence of the enlightened way she carried out her plans for reforms in full cooperation with the British, she was invested with the Order of the Star of India in 1872. She was informed about this in a letter from the Political Agent.

"It is with great pleasure that I have to send you my congratulations on this matter, that it has pleased Her Majesty on account of your hearty labours for the progress of your dominations, the redressing of grievances, advancement of your subject, and your loyalty to the British Government, which has been reported by the Government of India, to confer upon you of her Royal condescension the dignity of Knight Grand Commander of the Star of India, and has sent her commands to the Viceroy to confer on you the Star and the Insignia of the first class of this Exalted Order."[19]

The order was conferred during the Governor-General's durbar on November 16, 1872. The ceremony took place in Bombay, and Shah Jahan Begum travelled there with 276 persons which included her state officers, nobles and escorts.

The British were very fascinated by Shah Jahan Begam's character. She was very loyal to them like her mother. They also tried to show on many occasions that they too held the Begams administrative reforms in high esteem. Lord Lansdowne mentions Shah Jahan Begam's efforts in some detail.

"In the course of my tour, I visited no less than four Chiefs, and it would be ingratitude on my part if I did not acknowledge the warmth of the reception I met with at their hands, and I did not bear the testimony to the spirit of loyalty by which they were animated. I had the pleasure of visiting Her Highness the Begam of Bhopal, and I was astonished at her enlightenment, prudence, and ability. The loyalty of the state is proved both by its traditions and its history, and the Begam herself has always been a true friend and a firm supporter of the English throne. In spite of private sorrow, which at the time of my visit was weighing heavily upon her, her cordial and friendly welcome is something I shall not easily forget."[20]

In January 1878, when the Imperial Order of the Crown of India was first instituted, Shah Jahan Begam was along with the members of the Royal Family, appointed one of the ladies of that order. This in-itself is a proof of the good Anglo-Muslim relations which prevailed in Bhopal for nearly a century.

Shah Jahan Begam suffered from cancer on her left cheek. No doctor could cure her disease, and she died on June 16, 1901. Sultan Jahan Begam the fourth in the line of succession succeeded her mother immediately after her death.

NOTES

1. Mittal, Kamla, *op. cit.*, p. 27.
2. Sultan Jahan Begam, *Hayat-i-Shahjehans: Life of Her Highness the late Nawab Shah Jahan Begam*, Time Press, 1926, pp. 2-3. See *Begamat-e-Bhopal*, p. 77.

   Nawab Sikander Begam nursed her daughter herself, and bought her up under her own guidance. Although the present day system of child-training was not in vogue at that time, yet the princess received all the benefits that can be expected from the tutelage of an educated mother, whom nature had richly endowed with extraordinary intelligence, firmness and administrative talents. As the princess grew up, the Begam began to familiarise her with the domestic duties of a well regulated Indian Home. The services of Moulvi Haseeb Ahmad, Haji Abdul Karim Ansari and Moulvi Hyder Ali Khan (author of the *Muntahi-ul-Kalam*) a man famous for his piety and learning, were engaged for purpose of her general and religious education. Munshi Raza Husain, Assistant Muatamid-ul-Muham and Deewan Thakur Pershad, First Revenue Assistant to the Muatamid-ul-Muham, were ordered to instruct her in the elements of finance and revenue. Lessons were also given to her in riding and musketry, and in these, her ancestral accomplishments, she attained to great proficiency. In short, by virtue of her natural intelligence and constant application to her studies, the princess got through all the stages of her early education at a surprisingly rapid pace.

3. Mittal, Kamla, *op. cit.*, p. 29.
4. *Ibid.*
5. *Ibid.*
6. Begum, H.H. Nawab Sultan Jahan, *An Account of My Life*, Vol. 1, translated by C.H. Payne, London, 1910.
7. *Ibid.*, pp. 283-85. See also Mittal, Kamla, *op. cit.*, p. 31, Preckel, Claudia, *op. cit.*, pp. 121-22.
8. Bhopal Political Agency: File No. 1384/34 of 1888-95: Her Highness the Begam of Bhopals, Dictionary in six languages.
9. *Ibid.*
10. Nawab Sultan Jahan, *Hayat-i-Shajehani: Life of Her Highness the Late Nawab Shahjahan Begam of Bhopal*, C.I.G.C.S.I. (tr. by B. Ghosal), Bombay, Time Press, 1926, p. 86.
11. *Ibid.*
12. *Ibid.*
13. *Ibid.*
14. *Ibid.*, p. 80.
15. Preckel, Claudia, *op. cit.*, p. 121.
16. Shah Jahan Begam, Taj-ul-ikbal, p. 229.
17. Preckel, Claudia, *op. cit.*, p. 150.
18. Nawab Sultan Jahan, Hayat-i-Shahjehani, p. 69.
19. Nawab Sultan Jahan Begam, *Account of My Life*, Vol. 1, 265.
20. Nawab Shah Jahan Begam, *Taj-ul-Iqbal*, 170f.

15

Ashrafunnissa Begam

(1840—1903)

Ashrafunnissa Begam came from a family of a modest means, but interestingly one in which the women were traditionally taught to read, though never to write. They belonged to the Sayyeds family, the highest status group among the Ashrafs. Her father was a Vakil (legal practitioner), was employed in the Princely state of Gwalior, so Bibi Ashraf and her siblings grew up in her grandfather's house. As was the practice of the day a female teacher called ustani came to the house to teach the girls to read the *Quran*. Her grandmother also encouraged her to read the Holy Quran which she finally completed. She however could not still read Urdu which she wanted to so in order to participate in majalis—poetic recitations organised by the family. She asked a relative for the text of some of the poems offered on such occasion, claiming that she would have them copied so she could practice reading and reciting them. With great difficulty she copied the text and found a teacher—her cousin. Gradually she learned Urdu.[1]

At the age of nineteen Ashrafunnissa was married to a cousin, Sayyed Alamdar Husain, and moved to Lahore. Her husband was well educated. He had great command over western sciences and oriental literature through the medium of Urdu. He died in 1870 leaving Bibi Ashraf with two young daughters. She never remarried, but raised her children, educated them, and supported herself, first by taking in sewing and later by teaching at the Victoria Girls School in Lahore. She was a woman of tremendous determination, sustained by a firm religious faith. Her in-depth discussion of how she learned to read and write was published in 1899 in *Tahzib-un-Niswan*, an

Urdu newspaper for women published in Lahore. She passed away in 1903. The editor of the above newspaper, Muhammadi Begam, wrote a biography based on Bibi Ashrafi's own story that later became a source of inspiration to many students especially Muslim girls.

NOTES

1. Minault, Gail, *Secluded Scholars: Women's Education and Muslim Social Reform in Colonial India*, Oxford University Press, New Delhi, 1998.

16

Abadi Banu Begam

(1852—1924)

Abadi Banu Begam more popularly known as Bi Amman, belonged to an administrative family in the Muslim Princely state of Rampur. She had learned the Quran as a child and thus knew the Arabic script in a rudimentary fashion. She learnt Urdu by asking her nephew to read to her from a book of stories, committing it to memory, and then re-reading it herself, partly from memory and partly by sounding out the letters—since the script for Persian and Urdu was only slightly different from that of Arabic, she could read Persian also. She became a great story teller, but she never learned to write. Abadi Banu Begam was widowed young, with five sons and a daughter to raise. She never remarried, but following a common theme of self-sacrifice for the love of learning—she pawned her gold ornaments in order to ensure that her sons had a good education.[1]

NOTE

1. Minault, Gail, *Secluded Scholars: Women's Education and Muslim Social Reform in Colonial India*, Oxford University Press, New Delhi, 1998.

17

Nawab Sultan Jahan Begam

(1858—1930)

Nawab Sultan Jahan Begam was the last female ruler of Bhopal. After the death of her mother Nawab Shah Jahan Begam she became the full-fledged ruler of Bhopal state on 4 July, 1901. The coronation ceremony took place in Sadar Manzil palace. All the state guests, with the chief guest Col. Meade, assembled to celebrate, the coronation of the Nawab. At the time of her accession she was 43 years old. She received the Khilat from the British Government, at the investiture ceremony, two robes of honour, a pearl necklace, a tiara, a gun and a sword. The Khilat was valued at about ten thousand rupees. She was seated on the throne with 21-gun salute.

Early Years

Nawab Sultan Jahan birth was celebrated with great pomp and joy. This was very much unlike patriarchal Hindu families in India where the birth of the girl-child is looked down upon. Before she reached the age of two years, her grandmother Nawab Sikander Jahan Begam had been confirmed as the ruler of the state, and the law of succession had been established. In 1867, Nawab Sultan Jahan Begam's father Nawab Umrao Dula had died and after sixteen months of his death her grandmother, Nawab Sikander Jahan Begam also passed away. These tragedies took place in her family when she was only 10 years and 7 months. After the death of her grandmother she was totally under the care and supervision of her mother who looked after her early education. In her biography she writes that, "........... the foundation of my education was laid, with the customary invocation of the divine blessings. A regular course of study was prescribed for me, and my daily routine was as follows :

Before Noon

From 5 O'clock to 6	—	Open-air exercise
From 6 O'clock to 7	—	Morning meal
From 8 O'clock to 10	—	Study of the Quran
From 10 O'clock to 11	—	Breakfast with Nawab Sikander Begam
From 11 O'clock to 12	—	Recreation

Afternoon

From 12 O'clock to 1	—	Handwriting lesson
From 1 O'clock to 3	—	English lesson
From 3 O'clock to 4	—	Persian lesson
From 4 O'clock to 5	—	Arithmetic
From 5 O'clock to 5.30	—	Pashtu lessons and writing practice alternately
From 5.30 O'clock to 6	—	Riding lesson
From 6 O'clock to 7	—	Evening meal

And at 8 O'clock to Bed

The following were her teachers :

Study of the Quran	—	Hafiz Sayad Muhammad Surati
Translation and tafais of the Quran	—	Maulvi Jamat-ud-Din
Handwriting	—	Raza Ali Shirin Rakam
English	—	Munshi Husain Khan
Persian	—	Maulvi Bukhari
Arithmetic	—	Guru Ji Pandit Ganpat Rai
Fencing	—	Syed Amir Ali
Riding	—	Ustad Hakdad Khan
Pastu	—	Akhand Sahib

As a result of the good education she received under renowned teachers, Nawab Sultan Jahan Begam wrote her memoirs in three volumes[1] apart from this work, she also wrote a number of books discussing different aspects of human life, the book Al Hijab is one of them, which deals with the matter concerning purdah or veil system in ladies. Even though she was a great patron of purdah, and herself wore burqa, she did not see it as a symbol of segregation. She performed all her administrative duties behind the veil and also participated in state functions of the Government of India and elsewhere. She encouraged the authorities to arrange separately for ladies, so that they may freely move and perform any activities relating to the occasion without any inhibition. She also inaugurated purdah garden of Lady Hardinge Medical College at Delhi.

Nawab Sultan Jahan Begam was a great promoter of art. Her children also promoted it in their individual capacities. Nawab Sultan Jahan Begam patronized art and handicraft in her state and also outside her state. She attended many art exhibition held in different places in India, where the arts and handicraft from state girls school students and destitute women's institute were displayed and won many prizes for the state. She encouraged the teaching of art and handicraft in two popular girls' school in her state, viz. Sultania and Victoria Schools. She herself presented many handicrafts and paintings to her Excellencies and Queen of England. In her Account she wrote, "I have a taste for art ever since my childhood. In my early age, I found scope for this taste in excluding ornamental needle work of various kinds and particularly embroidery.[2]

Some of the significant reforms that were undertaken by her are as follows :

Educational Reforms

Nawab Sultan Jahan Begam genuinely wanted to improve the quality of education in her state. She is especially credited of establishing schools for both boys and girls. On 17th October 1903 a school called the Alexander school for sons of Sardars was founded. This was especially meant to educate the sons of Bhopal Jagirdars and high officials of the state along with her third son, Sahibzada

Hamidullah Khan. A school in Sehore was especially started for Muslim boys to teach them Quran. Further to promote Quranic education among them, she also instituted some scholarships.

One post of Director of Public Instruction was created in the year 1904-05 and the first D.P.I. appointed was Moulvi Abdul Ghafoor Shahbaz. Another school for boys in the Bhopal city was the Jahangiria School which was raised to the high school standard by Her Highness.[3]

In 1908, the Nawab Begam also sanctioned for the foundation of a middle school at each of the three tehsils—Baseli, Bairasia and Bamhori.

Some new regulations were framed in the year 1906-07 regarding education. Tuition fees was introduced in the city school but Her Highness exempted the village school from tuition fees.

In 1906, an educational code was drawn up by the Moien-ul-Moham, prior to that no set of regulations was in existence which could have served as a guide in matters of education under the old system the directions issued by the rulers or their minister were the only guide. Under the new code the high school had been affiliated to the Allahabad University and mathematics was made compulsory in schools. With regard to the oriental literature, the Punjab University course had been adopted.[4]

In her Account, she mentions that the state was spending ten thousand rupees every year on scholarships. Those scholarships were given to assist students qualify themselves in medicine, engineering, agriculture, law and other sciences, or to enable them to proceed to Europe for advanced study.

A significant feature of the state education worth mentioning was the provision in different classes of regular courses in moral and civic instruction, which aimed at inculcating in the student, at his or her most impressionable age, certain ideals of the character and more broadly still to initiate him or her in the knowledge of the common virtues and duties of civic life.

She is credited of establishing a library named Hamidia Library which was originally started in 1900 by her third son Sahibzada Hamidullah Khan. This became a source of instruction for the pupils and scholars of the state.

However, the most significant step that was undertaken by her in the field of education was regarding women's education. She was extremely keen to promote women's education because there was a realization on her part that social progress and for the well being of a family, education of women, was extremely essential. In her own words she writes:

> "It is perhaps forgotten that women, too, are half the community, and no real progress can be achieved if the educational needs of this important area is neglected and started of."[5]

In her mind she had already visualized an appropriate curriculum for female education and in this reference she mentions in her account:

> "In my opinion, imperfect education is worse than none at all. The sweet water of this spring should either be drunk deep or not tasted at all. It is a stupid thing to my mind, to teach the girls to read and write, and then leave them to their fate. The very least that should be done for them, is to give them a thorough grounding in things that matter, and to awaken the dormant soul in them."[6]

She further writes:

> "Although greatly handicapped by the absence of a well thought out curriculum, I made the best of my resources and made a start with a few classes in which the Holy Quran with its translation, Urdu, Arithmetic, Geography, and Domestic Economy were taught."[7]

It is true that the earlier Nawab of Bhopal were keenly interested in promoting women's education, however it was only Nawab Sultan Jahan Begam who introduced a curriculum especially for women that was scientific. She is credited of establishing a new institution for women with a new name, i.e. the "Sultania Girls School" in an annexe of the Taj Mahal, and closed conveyances were provided by the state to bring all the girls to the school in the morning and take them back in the afternoon.

Despite, the school being open for only women belonging to noble and rich families, it shows the genuine concern of the Nawab in promoting women's education in her state.[8]

In 1912, the Sultania Girl's School was affiliated with the middle school course of the University of Allahabad. According to Her Highness in her account she writes:

> "A special school was opened this year (15-6-1907) for the benefit of the Hindu Girls, whose claims on my attention were quite as insistent as those of their Mussalman sisters. The religious needs of Hindus being entirely different from those of the Mussalmans, and education divorced from religion being a thing of no value in my eyes. The school was named Birjisia Kanya Pathshala."[9]

Her deep concern for women's education was clearly reflected in a speech at the prize distribution ceremony at the Sultania Girls' School on 16 February, 1911:

> "Culture is the basis of civilization, and female education is the key to culture .... and now, my daughters, let me ask you to make the most of the opportunities that have been given to you. Seek diligently to acquire knowledge, which is a woman's wealth, and culture, which is her adornment, but do not forget that true comeliness consists in nobility of character. In this way you will grow up to be loved by old and young—misfortunes will be unable to crush you, and worldly prosperity will never make you proud. Remember that the object of your education is not that you may undertake the duties of me, but that you may acquire those womanly accomplishments and virtues which will enable you to become capable housewives and good mothers. The management of a home and the training of a child are two of the noblest and most responsible of human duties, and God created women for their performance ...."[10]

From the above speech it is clearly evident that Nawab Sultan Jahan Begam wanted to improve the quality of family life. She strongly believed that if women were educated they would become good mothers, virtuous wives who would also prove to be effective companions to their husbands. Further she did not want to link education always with professionalism, what she desired was to improve the thinking and attitude of women so that they can transmit values and culture effectively to their progeny and thus become effective agents of socialization.

In the year 1912, the state budget marked one lakh rupees per year for education and ten thousand for total scholarships.[11] Later on the amount was raised as she made some endowments for educational purposes.

Nawab Sultan Jahan Begam, in all, made three endowments for the permanent advancement of education within her state even after her death.[12]

The second endowment was made in August 1917 and the sum was 5,24,400 rupees and the Bilqisia Girls School was added to the institutions covered by the first endowment.[13]

Lastly in 1918, a separate endowment of the face value of four lakh rupees was raised for a similar purpose in respect of the boys school in Bhopal, known as the Sulemania and Jahangiria Schools.[14] It is significant to note that the Alexendra School, which was founded by the Nawab for the nobles' sons was combined with the Jahangiria School in 1923.

Nawab Sultan Jahan Begam was deeply concerned about the welfare of widows and destitute women in her state. As a result of her endeavour a school for widows and destitute women was established to teach them some useful professions like needle work, handicrafts, so that they may be able to earn an independent living. The institution for the widows and the destitutes was formally opened by Col. Obaidullah Khan, the second son of Her Highness on 23rd May, 1905.[15] The upkeep of this institution was maintained by royal donations and public subscriptions.

Besides the above mentioned schools, which were directly maintained by the Government, there were six public schools aided by the State Government, namely City Sanskrit Pathshala, the Jain

Digambar Pathshala, the Jain Shwetambar Pathshala, the Kanya Vidyalaya and the Sehore Kanya Pathshala.[16]

In 1911, a kindergarten class for the training of young children was opened in Bhopal. The class was held in the Ali Manzil.

In fact, under the reign of Nawab Sultan Jahan Begam female education made great progress. She was of the strong view that female education was of "vital importance for the progress and well being of my country."[17]

Medical Aid

Nawab Sultan Jahan Begam was fully committed in improving the health and overall care of women and children in her state. Two hospitals were established in Bhopal state, i.e. Prince of Wales Hospital for males and Lady Lansdowne Hospital for females. For infants—The Lady Hardinge Infant Home was maintained under the supervision of the Lady Lansdowne Hospital.[18]

The Infant Home and Lady Minto Nursing School was inaugurated by Lady Hardinge, during her visit to Bhopal in 1912.

Regarding, the necessity of a nursing school, Her Highness in her account mentions that :

> "In times of illness, we need not only good doctors and medicines, but good nursing. I know from my own experience how much patients suffer in this country in consequence of the ignorance which prevails of the art of nursing. In Europe, many women receive expert training in this art, which they practise as a profession. They are ready for service not only in hospitals and nursing homes, but in private houses. There is scarcely a woman in Europe who does not possess some knowledge of nursing. In India, unhappily, the reverse is the case. It is surely, therefore, a matter of the utmost importance that the steps should be taken to train Indian women as nurses, so that the people in every grade of society may be able to obtain the assistance, they so urgently need. It was with these thoughts in my mind that I determined to establish a school for nursing in Bhopal. As Her Excellency Lady Minto had done

> so much for the cause of nursing in India, I asked and obtained Her Excellency's permission to name the institution after her name. I called it, accordingly, the Lady Minto Nursing School, and a start was made on a small scale in the month of August, 1909."[19]

Some of the initial problems that were faced by the institution is vividly portrayed in her account :

> "It was no easy matter to find public (pupils) for the new school, but at length by dint of persuasion, the promise of scholarship, and a little gentle pressure, a class of girls between the ages of 10 and 12 was got together, and work was commenced. Instruction was imparted both in Urdu and in English. I made the school, a branch of the Lansdowne Hospital."[20]

She also opened a class for the instruction in midwifery. She called all the midwives in Bhopal and ordered them to attend daily at the Lady Lansdowne Hospital to receive instruction from the lady doctor. They were also ordered to send their daughters (as the profession of midwifery was hereditary) to the lady doctor for elementary training. A certificate was granted to every woman whom the lady doctor considered competent to undertake maternity cases; and the Nawab issued an order that only those who obtained such certificates were to practise as midwives, and that any woman contravening that order were to be punished. In order to make the scheme popular, she directed that every woman who attended the classes was to receive an allowance of five rupees a month. In her account, she writes:

> "In any State or Province, a system of medical relief which does not include the provision of trained nurses and midwives can benefit only half the population, since it leaves out of account the needs of the female sex."[21]

After a considerable time, a number of midwives and lady health visitors under medical department or health department became incharge of the work of the child and maternity welfare in the city.

Special measures were undertaken by the Public Health Department to eradicate smallpox, and to popularize the vaccination, a reward of four annas (25 paise) per child vaccinated was offered by Her Highness.[22]

It is very significant to note that during the reign of Nawab Sultan Jahan Begam the number of dispensaries in mofussils had increased. Sanitary officers were posted in all districts. Two new hospitals were opened in the southern and eastern districts, and competent staff was also provided.[23]

Administrative Reforms

The administrative reforms that were carried out by Nawab Sultan Jahan Begam deserves special mention. She was an enlightened ruler who wanted to help the poor and needy and punish the corrupt officials of the state. She sent her own son's to tour and extensively survey the status of the cultivators in her own provinces and in the rural areas. After getting the first hand account of their conditions, she tried to solve their problems. Generally honest officials in her state were rewarded and the guilty were punished. In the second year of her reign she herself toured the state and gained the first hand knowledge of her subject.

Effective steps were taken to modernize Bhopal's administration. Telephone connections were installed in the palace, administrative department of the state. Further on 1 July, 1908, Bhopal State Post Office was amalgamated with the Imperial Post Office of India. According to the terms of amalgamation the Imperial Post Office was also to supply the Bhopal Durbar Service stamps free of cost according to the actual requirement of the state.[24]

Reforms in Revenue Administration

Since land revenue was the chief income of the state, Nawab Sultan Jahan Begam made significant changes.

- The system of farming in village, which was abolished by late Nawab Sikander Begam was again introduced by Nawab Sultan Jahan Begam.

- In her times most of the land was under Revenue contractors or ijaradars. They were directly responsible to the state for the assessed revenue of the village they held. The responsibility of state officials and tehsildars was to see that only the assessed revenue was collected by the farmers. In bad years or when severe drought plagued the state-suspension and remissions were also freely made by the court.
- Land Revenue Act had been modified and passed into law.
- Two new training schools for patwaris were opened by the order of the Nawab Sultan Jahan Begam, and the Rules especially relating to these schools had been drawn up and approved by her. An agricultural farm had been opened by her under the supervision of the director of land records at village Sionia Ankara, Dewanganj tahsil. In her account she mentions that the farm was run on the most advanced scientific lines. In fact, it would serve as a model to the cultivator's who in the long run would emulate it.
- In 1910 the state sent a number of experienced and intelligent mustajirs to agriculture exhibition held at Lahore, in order that they might see the results of recent agricultural experiments, and become acquainted with latest technological advancements in implements used by the farmers.
- She established a district department to meet the needs of the state in the matter of irrigation because of the existing deficient rainfall in the state.
- Certain taxes that were unbearable by the cultivators were abolished.

Judicial Reforms

In her account Nawab Sultan Jahan depicts that, "The whole work of administration, the maintenance of order and security, the redress of wrongs, everything depends upon the law of the country, and upon what they are enforced."[25] In the beginning of her reign she created a separate post for judiciary and legislative head called

Nasir-ul-Moham. The legislative department was under the charge of Nasir-ul-Moham, who, in consultation with legislative committee drew up regulations for the chief's approval when approved by the Nawab these regulations had the force of law. According to Bhopal State Gazetteer, "The spirit of the British Codes and Acts is always followed, the laws themselves being suited to local requirements. The laws themselves serving Muhammadans and Hindus separately are based on the Quran and Dharamashastras, respectively.[26]

Nawab Sultan Jahan Begam had always paid special attention to the judicial department. The Nasir-ul-Moham (Minister for Judiciary) of the state possessed almost the same powers as those enjoyed by High Court, and in special cases under certain condition the final appeal was made to Nawab herself. But still there was some scope for further improvements, so that a High Court and a Judicial Council were established in the state in 1922. His Excellency Lord Reading, the Ex-Chief Justice of England, inaugurated the High Court of Bhopal State.[27]

Military Reforms

During the reign of Nawab Sultan Jahan Begam, the army of the state was remodelled out of the gangs of disorderly retainers, which were scattered all over the state. A regular force was constructed in which every man was the servant of the state and drew his pay directly from the state treasury. Also, the state artillery, which was ill-regulated and badly equipped, was thoroughly re-organized.

To make the functioning of military more effective in September 1904 she started a military school in order that the boys of the higher classes may acquire military training and come out of the institution as officers in the state army. The school however existed only for a period of five years. The irregular army wing called "Intizamia" was equipped in a native style. They carried messages and acted as police assisting district officers.

In the year 1903 the Nawab received Kharita from the British Government of India regarding the reorganisation of the Imperial Service Troops.

Nawab Sultan Jahan overhauled the army of the state with efficient men, good horses and new uniforms. The Imperial Service Troops or the State derived good name from the Delhi Durbar and also its good performance in South African campaign were also praised.

Police and Jail Reforms

A regular police force in the Bhopal state was first started in 1857, all watch and ward previous to this year was being done by the irregular army. These police were at first distributed through the city, the Kotwal, who was also a Magistrate, being incharge. Later on district police were introduced. In 1886, the police were re-organized and the Kotwal was replaced by a Muntazim at headquarters and inspector in each Nizamat.[28]

The administrative report of Bhopal state for the year 1904-05 confirms that the police force had been re-organized and reformed by Her Highness and was supervised by the Judicial Minister and the Superintendent was the Chief Executive Officer of the force whose sanctioned strength in the year 1960 was 2060 policemen and officers. Mounted police numbering 295 jawans and 58 officers were taken from the Bhopal army. Chief Inspector and facilities of proper training were provided to the men of the unit. This arrangement was made in the police force to facilitate the work of the police. The force was also supplied with fire-arms.[29]

The first jail in the state was established in 1899. Later a Central Jail was built in Bhopal city and four subordinate district jails were situated in the Nizamats.

Industrial Development in the State

Nawab Sultan Jahan Begam was keenly interested in promoting industrial development in her state. According to the Gazetteer of the year 1908, "the chief industries were weaving and printing of cotton cloth, the making of jewellery and preparation of 'gutka' a mixture of saffron, lime and other ingredients eaten with betel leaf, of which the Bhopal variety is famous. In her account, the Begam mentions that, "A cotton mill had been set up in Bhopal in my mother's reign, but it had never been in charge of an expert, nor had it been managed on sound business lines. It had, in consequence, never proved a profitable concern."[30]

She established a sugar factory on an experimental basis to promote the trade and industry in the state. In order to further expand trade in her state, Nawab Sultan Jahan Begam reduced the custom duties carried out this reform so that her dream of making Bhopal a flourishing trade centre was fulfilled.

To improve the local arts and manufactures many attempts were made by the Nawab. Art and craft were part of the school curriculum in most of the Girl School and orphanages that was established by the Nawab. Further, in 1908 two classes, one of tailoring and the other of boot making had been added to the Sulemania School. A student was also deputed to Lahore Industrial School.

It is significant to note that Bhopal was a great feeder of Bombay cotton trade to foreign country.

For promoting trade and commerce in her state industrial exhibitions were held from time to time. In the year 1908 with a view to promote the cause of trade, "a large fair was held in Shahjahanabad. Her Highness exempted all who opened stalls from the payment of Octroi duties on the commodities and animals they imported for sale.[31]

To promote home industry within the state, industrial schools were also opened in the city, where along with primary education, boys were taught the useful art of tailoring, carpentry, smith-work, cane work, etc.[32]

The Nawab opened a school for destitute women. She called it Asifia Technical School for Destitute Women. The handicraft made by women in this school won many prizes for Bhopal in All India exhibitions.

During the reign of Her Highness maximum construction work were carried on along with repairing and expansion of old buildings belonging to previous rulers; certain construction work was incomplete, e.g. Taj-ul-Masjid. As the Gazetteer indicates:

> "The department (Public Works Department) has done much excellent work; among the principal constructions during the last ten years are the water-works which supply the whole city and its suburbs, costing Rs. 18 lakhs, the Taj-ul-Masjid 16 lakhs, the large tent and furniture store house in Jahangirabad Rs. 23 lakhs, the Lansdowne hospital for women Rs. 28,000, the Imperial Service Cavalry Lines Rs. 5 lakhs, the new central jail Rs. 1.5 lakhs and metalled roads costing Rs. 18 lakhs. In 1905, Rs. 91,000 were expended on public works."[33]

Thus, under the reign of Nawab Sultan there was overall progress made in different fields in her state and region.

Nawab Sultan Jahan Begam abdicated the throne in favour of her third son Sahibzada Hamidullah Khan, because of the premature death of her two elder sons in 1924, including the recognized heir apparent Nawab Nasrullah Khan. The reason she gave for her abdication was clearly reflected in a speech which she delivered on the occasion of coronation ceremony of Nawab Hamidullah Khan. She stated that:

> "The last few years were the most tragic of my life, and they tested my endurance and my spirit of resignation of the Will of God to the utmost limit .... Nevertheless these sad misfortunes have affected my heart and mind, and I feared lest they might affect state affairs also, hence I decided to transfer the burden of responsibility to the shoulders of my successor, so that free from all duties of rule and government, I might denote myself to my prayers, and to the service of humanity, especially my own sex."[34]

Sultan Jahan Begam died on 14th May, 1930. Her death was in the newspaper—*Pioneer*, of 14th May 1930. It mentioned that, "Begam, Mother, the Nawab of Bhopal who was operated upon yesterday passed away just before mid-day today. Her end was peaceful and she was conscious to the last."[35]

Further the weekly paper *Naresh* from Lahore of 18th May, 1930 reported the last blessings and message she gave her son, "................ I am now departing from this world and I entrust you to the keeping of great Allah."[36]

The twenty-five years of her rule were eventfully and was marked by progress, prosperity and she strove hard to improve the status of women and girls in her state.

NOTES

1. Nawab Sultan Jahan Begam, *Hayat-i-Shahjehani: Life of Her Highness, the Late Nawab Shahjahan Begam of Bhopal*, p. 69.
2. Nawab Sultan Jahan Begam, *op. cit.*, Vol. II, p. 179.
3. Sultan Jahan Begam, *An Account of My Life*, Vol. II, Translated Abdus Samad Khan, Bombay, 1922. See also *Administrative Report, Bhopal State, 1905-06, 1906-07, 1907-08.*
4. Mittal, Kamla, *op. cit.*
5. Sultan Jahan Begam, *An Account of My Life*, II, 150ff.
6. *Ibid.*
7. Sultan Jahan Begam, *An Account of My life*, Vol. II, Translated by Abdus Samad Khan, Bombay, 1922, p. 152.
8. For details see *Bhopal State Administrative Report of the Year.* Preckel Claudia, *op. cit.*, pp. 182-83, Mittal, Kamla, *op. cit.*
9. Nawab Sultan Jahan, *op. cit.*, p. 265.
10. Sultan Jahan Begam, *op. cit.*, Vol. III, p. 121.
11. Claudia Preckel, *op. cit.*, p. 182.
12. Mittal, Kamla, *op. cit.*, p. 89.
13. *Ibid.*
14. Foreign and Political Department, Government of India, 1931, File No. 443-P, p. 6.
15. *Administrative Report*, Bhopal State, 1905 to 1908.
16. Mittal, Kamla, *op. cit.*
17. *Ibid.*
18. Mittal, Kamla, *op. cit.*, p. 89.
19. Nawab Sultan Jahan Begam, *op. cit.*, Vol. III, pp. 21-23.

20. *Ibid.*, p. 23.
21. *Ibid.*, pp. 25-26.
22. *Bhopal State Administrative Report*, 1905-06.
23. Nawab Sultan Jahan Begam, *op. cit.*, Vol. II, p. 253.
24. Mittal, Kamla, *op. cit,*, p. 39.
25. Nawab Sultan Jahan Begam, *op. cit.*, Vol. II, p. 139.
26. *Bhopal State Gazetteer*, pp. 61-62.
27. Mittal, Kamla, *op. cit.*, p. 57.
28. *Bhopal State Gazetteer*, III, p. 72.
29. Mittal Kamla, *op. cit.*, p. 64.
30. *Ibid.*, pp. 67-68.
31. *Ibid.*, p. 69.
32. *Ibid.*, p. 70.
33. *Ibid.*, p. 77.
34. *Ibid.*, p. 91.
35. *Ibid.*, p. 92.
36. *Ibid.*

18

Tayyiba Begam

(1873—1921)

Tayyiba Begam was the only daughter of Imad-ul-Mulk, who was a greater supporter of women's education. She was highly educated. She completed her First Arts (F.A.) exams in 1895, by studying privately. In 1896 she married a medical doctor in the Nizam's service. Her marriage did not hinder her studies. She completed her B.A. from Madras University in 1910, and became the first Muslim woman to do so. She knew Arabic, Persian, Urdu and was fluent in English as well.

She became member and founder of organisation that took up the cause of social upliftment of woman. In 1913, she founded the Anjuman-i-Khavatin-i-Islam (Muslim Ladies Association). In her speech before the first meeting of this anjuman, Tayyiba called upon her Muslim friends to raise funds to support schools for poor girls, to teach them skills such as handicrafts so that they might raise themselves out of poverty, and to propagate Islamic teachings among Muslim students.

In 1918, she was invited to address a women's educational conference in Bhopal that was presided over by Begam Sultan Jahan. In her address she emphasised that women education should be promoted by all Muslim women of means. The curriculum she emphasised should not ape western ideas and values but lay emphasis on Quran, Persian, Urdu, English and skills needed for running a household: cooking, sewing, embroidery, home nursing, hygiene, domestic economy and child care. She further emphasised that education should lead to physical, development of children, particularly girls. Provision of physical exercises, badminton and tennis should also be promoted.

Tayyiba Begam also presided over another educational conference, i.e. the All-India Muslim Ladies Conference in Calcutta in February 1919. At this conference she spoke not only of promoting girls education but also professional education of women, e.g. teachers, doctors and even typists. She also spoke of prevalent social evils in society, e.g. dowry and ill treatment of widows.

Tayyiba Begam was a prolific writer. Some of her works on fiction include a didactic story for children, *Hashmatunnissa*, and a social novel of Hyderabadi life, *Anwari Begam*. The latter was serialized in *Ismat* in 1909 and published later in a form of a novel.

Tayyiba passed away at the age of 48, in June 1921, after a prolonged struggle with breast cancer.[1]

NOTE

1. Minault, Gail, *Secluded Scholars: Women's Education and Muslim Social Reforms in Colonial India*, Oxford University Press, Delhi, 1998.

19

Rokeya Sakhawat Hossein

(1880—1932)

Rokeya Sakhawat Hossein was the first woman to launch a systematic and uncompromising campaign for women's education. She was born in a zamindar family in Payrabad, Rangpur in Bengal. She combined in herself the qualities of a writer, educationist and social worker. She was a visionary who worked unceasingly for female education which she considered was the first pre-requisite for the emancipation of women. As was the well established traditions of 18th and 19th century Rokeya was put in purdah from the age of five. In her own words she said that :

> "From the age of five I had to observe purdah and had to conceal myself even from women. Men were in any case not allowed free entry into the antahpur (inner house). I was too young to understand what all the fuss was about, yet I would have to conceal myself and observe strict purdah."[1]

Thus, the idea of going to the school was out of question. In her own words she states that :

> "I never entered the precincts of a girls school or college in my childhood. What little I have learnt was due to my older brother's love and care for my education .... Other relatives taunted us, but neither my brother nor I paid any heed to this."[2]

Shamsunnahar Mahmud, Rokeya's first biographer, paints a graphic picture of the scene :

> "Their father disapproved highly of Rokeya's learning English or Bengali. Brother and sister would wait for nightfall .... would gather their books, and as darkness engulfed the world, a dim light would be lit in the youngster's rooms. By candlelight the brother taught while the sister drank deep at the fountain of knowledge."[3]

Rokeya learnt Bengali from her older sister, Karimunnessa, and English from her husband, Sakhawat Hossein. Rokeya dedicated Volume II of her book "Motichoor" to Karimunnessa, who was herself a poet.

Rokeya's work place was Calcutta where she founded the Sakhawat Memorial Girls' School in 1911. This was considered to be her major achievement because the school was an integral part of her ceaseless campaign for the education of Muslim girls and their journey out of (*abarodh*) inner space. At first, the medium of instruction in her school was Urdu. (Rokeya lamented the fact that she could not start a Bengali section even fourteen years after the founding of her school.)

In order to make her school popular among the Muslim section of the population, she had to go from door to door, entreating guardians to send their wards to schools, guaranteeing security and purdah by offering covered transport for the girls. The students recalled the phaeton (horse-drawn carriage) and motor-bus which took them to school. The school went a long way in legitimizing formal education for girls. At the Bengal Women's Education Conference in 1926 she delivered the presidential address :

> "The opponents of female education say that women will become wanton and unruly. Fie! They call themselves Muslims and yet go against the basic tenet of Islam which gives women an equal right to education. If men are not led astray once educated, why should women?"[4]

Rokeya strongly believed in women's emancipation. She also believed in equal right for women in the educational, economic and political spheres. That alone would ensure a just society where men and women could work side by side in harmony and peace. In fact, she was the first Muslim woman of Bengal who raised issues on gender exploitation and women's rights. This is clearly reflected in her writings, especially in '*Stree Jatin Abanati*' (The Degraded Condition of Women) and in *Ardhangi* (His Other Half).

The school which she had opened had a host of well-wishers, male and female, though orthodox opinion did its best to discredit Rokeya's efforts and threw aspersions on the women who attended the school. However, men and women from the Brahman, Hindu and Muslim communities from all over India congratulated Rokeya and gave her their support. Liberal dailies and periodicals such as the *Mussulman*, and *Amrita Bazar Patrika*, *Mohammadi Saugat*, and even *Al-Eslam* supported the cause of women's education.

In fact, Rokeya followed the footsteps of the great Bengali reformers like Raja Rammohan Roy and Iswhar Chandra Vidyasagar. In the words of Abdul Mannan Syed :

> "Pragmatism and secularism in place of spiritualism, individualism in place of emotionalism a spirit of critical enquiry in place of unquestioning acceptance of tradition and authority—Rokeya was an epitome of these renaissance traits."[5]

Apart from establishing formal schools for girls Rokeya was a prolific writer. She started her literary career in 1901 when her essay *Pipasha* (The Thirst) appeared in *Nabaprabha*. Her next piece *Alankar na Badge of Slavery* (Jewellery or Badge of Slavery) created a stir. It was published in a Journal *Mahila* (1310 B.S./ 1903). Her only English work was *Sultana's Dream.* Her only novel *Padmarag* (1924) is a narration of life in Tarini Bhavan, a sanctuary where women of all creeds have found refuge and live a life of dignity. The contemporary periodical *Samyabadi* in its Falgun 1331 B.S. (1925) issue reviewed *Padmarag* and recommended it to 'every man and woman' to read.

She was awarded an honorary degree in Persian by Calcutta University, and later became an examiner of MA degree in Persian at this institution.

NOTES

1. Ray, Bharati, *From the Seams of History: Essays on Indian Women*, Oxford University Press, New Delhi, 1995.
2. *Ibid.*, p. 117.
3. *Ibid.*, p. 118.
4. *Ibid.*, p. 121.
5. *Ibid.*, p. 122. See also Minault, Gail, *op. cit.*, pp. 261-262.

20

Masuma Begam

(1902—1990)

Masuma Begam was born in Hyderabad. She was the eldest daughter of Tayyiba Begam Khediv Jang, and hence the grand-daughter of Sayyid Husain Bilgrami. Her family strictly observed purdah. Her mother, though highly educated, observed purdah all her life. Masuma and her sisters all attended Mahbubiya Girls' School. In 1922, Masuma married her Oxford-educated cousin, Husain Ali Khan, who later on chaired the English Department at Osmania University. After her marriage Masuma's break from purdah came gradually. She recounted that her husband introduced her first only to his close personal friends. Later, they would go out to 'mixed' parties, but on such occasions, one could always inquire who was invited, and the wife could stay home if there were men invited who were not among her husband's circle of friends.[1]

Masuma continued to wear burqa in public in Hyderabad until Indian Independence. She was involved in the educational and social work among poor women that had been initiated by the mother.

She was the first and only Muslim lady to be a minister in Indian history. Her matchless record of meritorious service to the nation in more than one capacity, ever since 1921, is worth noting.

She was well-versed in the administration of democratic institutions. She was politically active and by 1952, she was well enough recognised as a civic figure. The Congress party offered her a ticket to contest the first general elections for the State legislature. The party gave her a constituency in heart of the old city of Hyderabad, where she canvassed from house to house early in the morning. She won the elections and went on to serve two terms. She proved her capability when she was appointed Minister for Social Welfare and Muslim Endowments. In 1957 she became the Deputy Leader of the Congress Legislative Party, and a Minister in the Andhra Pradesh cabinet in 1960.

Masuma Begum was associated with the All India Women's Conference since 1927. She also held prestigious office as a member of this conference. She held the position of Vice-President twice and in 1962 was elected President of the All India Women's Conference. She was elected Member-in-Charge-International Relations in 1957 and she played a conspicuous role in strengthening A.I.W.C.'s ties with foreign organisations.

In 1955 she led the A.I.W.C. delegation to the Golden Jubilee Congress of the International Alliance of Women—Colombo. In 1956, she was the Deputy Leader of the delegation that went to Russia and in 1959, she was elected member of the Interim Committee of the United Nations at its Second Conference of Non-Governmental Organisations held in Geneva. In the same year she led the delegation of the A.I.W.C. to Yugoslavia. She also led a delegation to Indonesia.

Masuma Begum was connected with many organisations. In 1966, she was appointed Chairman of the Central Social Welfare Board. She was the President of the Hyderabad Branch of the A.I.W.C., President of Anjuman-e-Khawateen and Lady Hydari Club and a Patron of the A.I.W.C. She was a member of the Managing Committee of the Red Cross.

Masuma was a fine orator and she could deliver debates and lectures with great wit and charm. She was a scholar in Persian language and literature. She also had a fair for Urdu and English. Apart from her passion for welfare work, she liked to read and write, and often broadcasts talks.[2]

NOTES

1. Basu, Aparna, Ray, Nandita, Jerry, Narasimhan, Diamond Jubilee, 1927-87, All India Women's Conference, New Delhi, Mahila Press (A.I.W.C.), New Delhi, 1987.
2. Minault, Gail, *Secluded Scholars: Women's Education and Muslim Social Reform in Colonial India*, Oxford University Press, New Delhi, 1998.

21

Rashid Jahan

(1905—1952)

Rashid Jahan was the eldest daughter of Sheikh Abdullah of Aligarh and Wahid Jahan Begam. She had the fortune of growing up in a home where all the women were involved in educational and literary pursuits. Her mother and aunt taught at the Aligarh Girls' School and wrote for Urdu magazines, including their own journal *Khatun.*

She received her formal education at Aligarh Girls' School and stood out as bold and outspoken. She acquired her higher education from Isabella Thoburn College at Lucknow where she studied Science. Here she distinguished herself as the author of short stories in Urdu and English. These were later published in the college literary magazines. Later Rashid Jahan entered Lady Hardinge Medical College in Delhi in 1924. She completed her medical degree in 1929 with specialization in obstetrics and gynaecology and joined the U.P. medical service. This once again took her back to Lucknow.

While pursuing her career in medicine she organized with her fellow medical students literacy classes and free medical clinics for the poor women of the city.

Having attended formal institutions of learning since her childhood day, Rashid Jahan did not observe purdah strictly. In her college days leaving Aligarh to go to college she observed purdah or (burqas) and going to the railway station at Aligarh, but once in train and away from home, they took them off.

After joining the medical service at Lucknow she came in contact with politically conscious young Urdu writers like Sajjad

Zaheer, Ahmad Ali and Sahibzada Mahmuduzzafar. The latter was the son of Dr. Saiduzzafar, Principal of the Lucknow Medical College and also belonged to a distinguished family from Rampur.

These writers were devoted to Indian nationalism and socialist revolution. This influenced their writings also. Rashid Jahan's writings also evolved in a similar direction. In addition, her medical practice brought her into contact with women of all classes, and her writings constantly reflected her active social conscience and compassion for the oppressed women.

She along with her friends decided to publish a collection of short stories reflecting their social and political concerns. The result was *Angare* ('Sparks' or 'Embers', 1932). This work later paved the way for the Urdu Progressive Writers Movement. Rashid Jahan also contributed to the volume. Her two contributions were—*Dilli Ki Sair* (A Visit to Delhi) and *Parde Ke Piche* (Behind the Veil), portrays women's plight with great economy and irony. The stories in the volume were especially designed to challenge conservative social conventions and orthodox religious opinion. The authors sought to set new trends in literature which was different from romantic and sentimental works. They wanted to highlight through their writings the problems of social inequality, life of the oppressed including labourer and women.[1]

Rashid Jahan's participation with Angare group identified her as a rebel, a symbol of emancipated women among the progressives and liberals, and for the conservatives, an example of what can happen if women were educated and freed from the seclusion of purdah.

She got married to Mahmuduzzafar in 1934. After her marriage she continued to practice medicine throughout 1930s and 40s. She continued to write short stories, radio plays and was active in the All-India Progressive Writers Association. Her literary output was pathbreaking. She died with cancer in 1952.

Rashid Jahans stories appeared posthumously. Her stories are noted for portraying social themes. They mainly revolve around women in the family and in society. In course of her profession she encountered many women who suffered from gross neglect especially from gynaecological diseases. They generally relied upon bogus cures. These problems faced by Muslim women were intricately woven in most of her short stories. .

Rashid Jahan's stories inspired many women of her times especially, Ismat Chughtai who later began as a writer of great repute.[2]

NOTES

1. Minault, Gail, *Secluded Scholars: Women's Education and Muslim Social Reform in Colonial India,* Oxford University Press, New Delhi, 1998.
2. *Ibid.*

22

Fazilatunnessa Zoha

(1905—1976)

Fazilatunnessa Zoha came from an ordinary family in Tangail, in Bengal. She passed the Matriculation Examination from Eden college in 1921, with flying colours. Later she completed her Bachelor's degree from Bethune College in Calcutta, and thus became the first Muslim woman to receive a Bachelor's degree and, subsequently, a Master's degree in mathematics from the Dhaka University. Fazilatunnessa was the first Muslim woman to study at this university for higher education. Her result in the M.A. examination in 1927 created a stir in all the circles. Nasiruddin, the editor of the progressive periodical *Saugat* (which upheld the cause of women's emancipation and awakening), arranged a reception for Fazilatunnessa in Calcutta, disregarding the constant opposition put up by the oxthodox quarters which did not want a woman to be accorded a 'public' reception. Fazilatunnessa also chose education for a career. She was the Head of the Department of Mathematics at the Bethune College in Calcutta, and later its Vice-Principal till 1947. This achievement of her's especially in the professional front was a rare honour for a Muslim woman to become a Vice-Principal in a premier educational institution in those days. In 1947, her family opted for Pakistan and Fazilatunnessa came to Dhaka and took charge of Eden College as its Principal.[1]

NOTE

1. Ray, Bharati (Ed), *From the Seams of History: Essays on Indian Women*, Oxford University Press, New Delhi, 1995.

23

Shamsunnahar Mahmud

(1908—1964)

Shamsunnahar Mahmud, was a writer, educationist, teacher, social worker, and later, a parliamentarian in East Pakistan. She was born in an enlightened family of Noakhali which had taken to western liberal education and government employment very early and had crusaded for women's rights. Her maternal grandfather, Maulana Abdul Aziz, was one of the founding members of the Muslim Suhrid Sammelani. Nonetheless, her childhood was spent in purdah in Chittagong. Later she received formal instruction and successfully acquired a number of degrees. At the age of nine she was taken out of Khastagir's Girls' School in Chittagong in order to observe purdah. In her reminiscences of her school day she writes:

> "What a vast institution, and how large the number of students. And of these only three or four were Muslims, no more .... The daughters of many illustrious families—Amiyamakha, the elder sister of the revolutionary Kalpana Dutta, and the sister of Deshpriya Jotindramohan Sen, studied there .... I had gone up to class VI when the issue of purdah was brought up. At the age of nine .... I was taken out of the school so that purdah would not be violated."[1]

Later she started her study under a male Hindu tutor at home. She describes how a thick curtain separated her from her tutor. This was a measure consciously taken by her parents to seclude her from her tutor. Despite, these strict measures of seclusion she passed her Matriculation Examination with excellent marks.

She was admitted to the Diocesan College in Calcutta to pursue her higher education. She did very well and secured the twentieth place among all the students who had appeared for the Intermediate Arts Examination under Calcutta University in 1928. She obtained her Bachelor's degree with distinction in 1932 and was accorded a civic reception by the Rokeya's Anjuman-i-Khawnateen-i-Islam the same year. In her address Rokeya said:

> "We are assembled here on the occasions of Nahar's passing her B.A. .... This is an honour for all of us women .... I pray that more women follow Nahar's footsteps."[2]

At the initiative of A.K. Fazlul Huq, the Chief Minister of Bengal at the time, Lady Brabourne College was set up in Calcutta in 1939 for the education of Muslim girls. Shamsunnahar accepted the post of a teacher in Bengali at the College in the same year. In 1942, even as the World War II raged and Bengal was in the middle of the Quit India Movement, Shamsunnahar appeared for the Master's examination as a private candidate.

Shamsunnahar was also a great writer. Her first work *Punyamayee* (The Virtuous Women) was published in 1925, when she was only seventeen. This book contains short biographies of eight great women of the Muslim world who served as role models. Among them were the mystic, Rabeya, the Prophet's daughter Fatema, and his wives, Ayesha and Khadija. *Begam Mahal* (The Queen's Quarters) was another well known work of hers. It recorded the lives of great Pathan and Mughal women of medieval India. But her most renowned book was the biography of Rokeya Sakhawat Hossein, her mentor and comrade in the crusade for women's education. *Rokeya Jibani* (The Life of Rokeya), was published from Calcutta in 1937.

Shamsunnahar was primarily an educationist and much of her writings is concerned with various aspects of education in Bengal (primary education, Bengali Muslim Women's education, etc.). In

1933, she and her brother Habibullah Bahar jointly brought out the progressive periodical *Bulbul* from Calcutta.

NOTES

1. Ray, Bharati (Ed), *From the Seams of History: Essays on Indian Women*, Oxford University Press, New Delhi, 1995, pp. 122-124.
2. *Ibid.*, p. 124.

24

Begum Sharifa Hamid Ali

Begum Sharifa Hamid Ali was born in a Muslim family well known for its progressive outlook. She grew up to be an ardent nationalist and a great champion of Hindu-Muslim unity. She was well-versed and proficient in Urdu, Persian, Gujarati, English, Marathi and French. Some of her hobbies were drawing, painting and music.

She was married to Hamid Ali, I.C.S. Officer. It is significant to note that even after her marriage she was able to give full time to her linguistic abilities, interest in music and social work. In 1907, she attended the session of the Indian National Congress from which she came away actively interested in the Swadeshi Movement and for uplifting the lot of Harijans. She also helped in starting nursing centres and classes for village women, constantly giving them every possible practical help and guidance.[1]

As a member of the All India Women's Conference, Begum Hamid Ali started branches in several places. While doing propaganda for the Sarda Act to raise the age of marriage of girls, she organized a special campaign in which Muslim women signed a petition asking that the Sarda Act be made applicable to Muslim marriages also. She also brought out a "Nika namesh" for Muslim women which has since been in use all over India and is recognized in the State Law Courts.

Begum Ali was, in turn, Honorary Treasurer, Chairwoman, Vice-President and President (1940) of the A.I.W.C. She was also Chairwoman of the Governing Body of the All India Women's Education Association. In 1933, she went to London as one of the three women representatives to the Round Table Conference where she gave evidence on behalf of women before the Joint

Parliamentary Committee in favour of equal franchise rights between men and women. In 1934, she represented the A.I.W.C. at the Istambul Congress of the International Alliance of Women and in 1937 at the Lohacovice (Czechoslovakia) Congress of the Women's International League for Peace and Freedom

In recognition of her long career of social service, the Government of India appointed her as the Indian representative on the U.N. Commission on the Status of Women. She was also a member of the National Planning Commission of the Indian National Congress and also a member of the Hindustan Textbook Committee.[2]

NOTES

1. Basu, Aparna, Ray, Nandita, Jerry, Narasimhan, Diamond Jubilee, 1927-87, All India Women's Conference, New Delhi, Mahila Press (A.I.W.C.), New Delhi, 1987.
2. Srivastava, Gouri, *Women Who Created History*, NCERT, New Delhi.

25

Begam Shaista Suhrawardy Ikramullah

Begam Shaista Suhrawardy Ikramullah had the fortune of growing up in a privileged educated family. Her mother a granddaughter of Nawab Abdul Latif, was a leader in the literary and cultural awakening of Calcutta Muslims in the nineteenth century. Her own father was a son of Ubaidullah-al-Ubaidi Suhrawardy, and a British trained doctor who served as a district medical officer with the railways and later in life became Vice-Chancellor of Calcutta University. Shaista Ikramullah mother though was educated observed purdah strictly. Her father, on the other hand, with his education in England, was considerably more westernised.

Shaista had the fortune of growing up in both the world, i.e. the world of purdah and the western style of living. Since her childhood she studied the Quran at home, learned to read both English and Urdu. She was fortunate of attending the convent school. It is interesting to note that she wore the uniform frock at the school, and put on her Indian dress at home. In her own words she stated that, "I spent my childhood and early girlhood between the Arabian Nights world of my mother's family, and my ultra-westernised home and the English school. This dual existence did not seem to have worried me, and I used to ship easily from one to the other, as I can still do . . . ."[1]

In fact, Begam Shaista Suhrawardy Ikramullah was in purdah from the age of nine until her marriage at eighteen to a member of Indian Civil Service, whose family originated in Bhopal. Her mother-in-law feared that having an exposure with western system of education Shaista would not adjust to household chores. However, she later realized her folly and misgivings which she had towards Shaista. On the other hand Shaista could well adjust into her husband's family because for her training in her mother's more traditional family. She and her husband—who was keen on having an educated wife—moved to New Delhi in the early 1930. It was at Delhi that she made her debute into civil service society at a huge garden party given by a high government official. In her own words she stated that:

> "........ I did not enjoy my first experience of being out of purdah at all. I felt embarrassed at being looked at by hundreds of men (while) decked up all in my best, and my enjoyment of the party was further spoiled by my having to spend the entire evening trying to avoid being seen by my uncle, who very strongly disapproved of my coming out of purdah."[2]

She continued to live between the two worlds of Anglo-Indian official life and the Muslim culture of families in Old Delhi, with whom she mixed. She also became acquainted with a number of Muslims who were active in politics, including the lawyer and the Congress member, Asaf Ali and his Bengali wife, Aruna. Shaista was from a political family and was sympathetic to nationalism. As a young girl at Calcutta, she attended women's meetings and even made speeches in one of them. However, during her early years she was not actively associated with the freedom struggle.

In 1930, she had gone to London along with her husband where she completed her Ph.D. In 1940, when she returned to India she was involved in organising the Muslim Women Students Federation and the Women's Sub-committee of the Muslim League. She was subsequently elected a Muslim League member of the Indian Constituent Assembly in 1946. Following partition in 1947, she became a member of the Constituent Assembly of Pakistan and served for seven years, as well as representing Pakistan at the U.N.

Throughout her autobiography, Begam Ikramullah portrays herself as doing what was expected of her in conditions of tremendous and rapid change. In fact her family background and education helped her to bridge the difference in her world (i.e. traditional and modern).

NOTES

1. Minault, Gail, *Secluded Scholars: Women's Education and Muslim Social Reform in Colonial India*, Oxford University Press, New Delhi, 1998, pp. 280-281.
2. Ray, Bharati (Ed), *From the Seams of History: Essays on Indian Women*, Oxford University Press, New Delhi, 1995.

26

Ismat Chughtai

(1915—1991)

Ismat Chughtai was the best known author of modern Urdu stories. She was born into a large middle-class Muslim family in 1915, and was ninth of the ten children. Her father, Qasim Beg Chughtai, was a civil servant in Uttar Pradesh, and the family moved frequently. Ismat and her sister were taught Urdu and the Quran at home by an ill-tempered ustani (teacher), whom Ismat disliked.

Ismat had a formal education in Aligarh and Lucknow. In Aligarh she did her middle school and her higher education that is college education at the Isabella Thoburn College in Lucknow. Here she was awarded a B.A. degree in 1938. When she was in her teens, her father died, and her family had to move to Jodhpur, where her uncle was Inspector-General of Police. She used to commute from home and school by train. She was a rebel from a very young age, Ismat took off her burqa in the train. Her uncle, saw her arriving in Jodhpur unveiled, questioned her, but she replied that she never listened to anyone—except her father and by then he was gone.[1]

In college, she refused to wear either a burqa (veil) or a chadar. Her uncle often threatened to marry her off, but she held out for further education, and argued that she needed to teach in order to support the children of one of her siblings, who was ailing. She decided to go back to Aligarh in 1938 for teacher training since there she could live with her relatives, but even then no training classes for women were offered at Aligarh. She was prepared to attend classes with men, but several other women students were not willing, so as a compromise they persuaded the principal of the men's training college to screen off part of the classroom so that women students could attend lectures. Ismat earned her BT (Bachelor of Teaching) in 1939. Thereafter, she taught in schools, and later on became an inspectress of municipal girl's schools in Bombay.

Ismat was a great writer. Her first published work was *Fasadi*, (The Trouble Maker) that appeared in the literary journal *Saqi* in 1938. Thereafter, she published several short stories, but the work that earned her a lot of fame, was *Lihaf* (The Quilt) that appeared in *Adab-i-Latif* in 1942, just two months before her marriage to Shahid Latif, a Bombay film writer and director. *Lihaf* caused a furor, for it was a frank treatment, not only of a wife's sexual frustration, but also of that woman's relationship with a female servant with whom she finds emotional companionship. This theme taken up by her was too much even for a progressive public opinion at the time. The journal was inundated with letters of protest. Ismat was unaware of the controversy until her marriage, at which point the journal sent her copies of the critical letters, assuming—apparently that now that she was married, she was mature enough to deal with them. Later Ismat was prosecuted by the Punjab government for obscenity, though the charges were ultimately dismissed.

The uproar over *Lihaf* and the subsequent trial did not discourage her from writing. She continued to publish short stories and novels based on the middle class women's existence, in a style that was frank, earthy, and colloquial. She was also a part of the Progressive Writers Association and wrote the script for the powerful film *Garam Hawa*. In her novel like *Tanhai Ka Zaher* she highlighted the plight of lonely elderly women, who are no longer wanted by their family. She also wrote about some of the social problems plaguing women. She wrote about the marginalized, and about prostitutes and "fallen" women, without condescension and with rare understanding. She won the Iqbal Sammelan and Soviet Land Nehru Award. She also acted in Shashi Kapoor's film *Junoon*.

She maintained that her life proved that: "If you were bold enough, you could do anything you liked." Ismat might have defied social conventions and narrow-mindedness in her life, but the theme of her stories are neither grandly political nor social-reformist. In fact, they treat the everyday struggles and rebellions of ordinary but original people especially women.

NOTE

1. Minault, Gail, *Secluded Scholars: Women's Education and Muslim Social Reform in Colonial India*, New Delhi, 1998.

27

Begam Akbar Jehan

(1916—2000)

Begam Akbar Jehan popularly known as "Madr-e-Meharban" (benign mother) shot into prominence when she spearheaded the "Quit Kashmir" movement with her husband Sheikh Abdullah who was lodged in prison by the erstwhile Maharaja of the State Hari Singh.[1]

She was born in a Gujjar family in 1916. Her father was a rich British businessman. Begam Jehan was a freedom fighter who had carved out a place for her in the socio-political life of the state.

Her ability to mobilize people came to the fore during "Quit Kashmir" movement and subsequently when her husband was in prison in 1946-47 as she came out of the confines of home and visited villages of the state to burn the "lamp of hope" for the oppressed people. During Sheikh Abdullah's imprisonment she received Mahatma Gandhi in Srinagar during the latter's visit to the state.[2]

Her efforts to provide solace to the victims of the 1947-48 Indo-Pak conflict when Pakistani raiders attached Kashmir earned her a special word from Lady Edwina Mountbatten for her "human touch". Though she always played a supporting role to her husband in politics, her political acumen came to light in 1971 when she spearheaded the campaign for independent candidate Shamim Ahmed Shamim against heavy weight Bhakshi Ghulam Mohammed, a former Prime Minister of the State and Congress candidate for the Srinagar parliamentary constituency. Shamim won the election.

During the prolonged incarceration of her illustrious husband, Begam Abdullah discharged the onerous responsibility of bringing up her children with remarkable courage and fortitude.

After the Indira-Sheikh Accord in 1975, she secured the mandate from her party and was elected to the Lok Sabha from Srinagar in 1977.

Her pioneering role in the uplift of women in Jammu and Kashmir was yet another facet of her personality.

Dominating the social life in Kashmir for over half a century, she remained closely associated with Markaz-e-Behbood-e-Khawateen (Women Welfare Centre) for the upliftment of the women folk.[3]

NOTES

1. *Nation and the World*, 16th August, 2000, p. 57.
2. *Hindustan Times*, July 11, 2000.
3. *The Times of India* News Service, July 11, 2000.

28

Begam Abida Ahmed

(1923 ....)

Begam Abida Ahmed was born on 17th July, 1923 in Hardoi district of Uttar Pradesh. Her father Mohammad Sultan Hyder Josh was an educationist and a social worker. She studied upto B.A. level and was an ardent social worker.

She held many political posts and was a member of several committees. In 1981-84 she was a member of the seventh Lok Sabha and she got elected on Congress-I ticket from Bareilly in Uttar Pradesh. From the same constituency she was re-elected to the eighth Lok Sabha. She was a member of the Estimates Committee and was also a former member of the National Integration Council, New Delhi.

She was also a leader of the Indian Women's Delegation to World Conference on the "Year of the Child" held in Moscow in 1979.

She was a great patron of India-Tunisia Friendship Association and was the Former Chairman of Ghalib Institute and Museum. She was a Chairperson of Indo-Bhutan Friendship Association and Indo-Czechoslovakia Cultural Association, and also patron of Unity International, Hakim Ajmal Khan Girls' School, New Delhi. She was a member of the governing body of Kalindi College, South Delhi Polytechnic for Women, New Delhi, "Roshni", Society for the Welfare of Women and Children, she was a former founder and Chairman of Mahila Imdad Committee, Balika Chaman (Home for destitute girls), Ghalib Institute.[1]

She was also a former Deputy Director-General, All India Women's Voluntary Services.

NOTE

1. Jain, C.K., *Women Parliamentarians in India*, Surjeet Publications, New Delhi, 1993.

29

Nargis

(1929—1981)

Nargis was born in Calcutta on June 1, 1929. Her mother Jaddan Bai, was an eminent singer from Punjab who grew up in Allahabad. Her father Mohan Babu was a Mahyal Brahmin from Punjab. He converted himself to Islam and assumed the name of Shri Abdul Rashid.

Nargis early education began in Bombay. She was enrolled in one of Bombay's well run private schools, Queen Mary's where she took to reading as a matter of habit. She was well read. The books she read was Kazantzabis, John Galbraith, Martin Luther King and Maulana Azad. Although she did not go to college after passing the Cambridge Certificate (school leaving) examination, she acquired the sophistication and airs of a well groomed young lady.[1]

The first film she acted as a child star was Talashe Haqim in which her mother played the leading female role. She appeared under the screen name of Baby Rani. The name Baby stuck to her thereafter as her personal pet name. Relatives, friends and close associates would call her Baby well into her middle age. The other significant movie which she acted in her teens was Taqdeer. Mehboob the director of the movie named her as Nargis. In fact, she was known as Nargis throughout her life. The film was released in 1943. Hardly had Taqdeer finished than she signed up with Fazli Brothers Films for a film called Ismat (1944). Some of her box-office hit films were Andaz and Barsaat (1949), Awaara (1951) and Shree 420 (1955). In fact Awaara became an international favourite with the audience. However, her best picture was Mother India in 1958 and Jogan in 1950. She acted in more than fifty films. She married Sunil Dutt in 1958.

Nargis Dutt travelled widely. She organized and participated in the shows for Ghalib Centenary in London; put up shows to collect funds for Bihar flood victims in Kuwait and the United Kingdom.

Nargis Dutt was the first lady of the film world to be awarded "Padamshree" in 1959. She also received award for her best performance in "Mother India" from Karlovy Vary Film Festival, Czechoslovakia and from Peru and Greece and Urvashi from President of India for her acting in 'Rat Aur Din'.[2]

In April, 1980 she was nominated to the Rajya Sabha and in the same year she became member of the Committee on Petitions.

She was an organizer, patron and member of several societies. Some of them are mentioned below:

She organized Amber Flow Ball for Defence of India during Chinese aggression. She organized and participated in the show for Ghalib Centenary in India. She was the patron of The Spastic Society, Bombay and Rang Kala Manch, Bhopal. She was the President of Central Bombay Bharat Scouts and Guides District Association, was Chairman of the Meena Kumari Charitable Trust for the Blind; was the Vice President of the Ajanta Arts Welfare Troupe—an organization that was founded by Shri Sunil Dutt (her husband) for entertaining Defence Personnel (including wounded officers and jawans) especially after the Indo-Chinese aggression in 1962. She was the Director of Uttar Pradesh Chal Chitra Nigam Limited, Lucknow and was a member jury, Children's Films Moscow, was a jury at the Karlovy Vary, International Film Festival.

She was credited of reconstituting the Children's Film Society, Delhi. She was also the life member of the following—Federation for the Welfare of the Mentally Retarded (India), New Delhi. She was also the Honorary Member, Bombay Panel for recommending entries to the International Film Festival in 1975.

Nargis and her husband Sunil Dutt were close friends of the Nehru's.

Her eventful life came to an end as she suffered from the cancer of the pancreas. She was treated in New York and in India, however despite good treatment she passed away on 3rd May, 1981. She was only fifty-two, in the prime of her post-cinema public career. Most of the leading newspapers in their headlines mentioned that, "Nargis: So ends the legend, last journey of a queen, A time for farewell, salute to the Lady in White, End of an Era." The *Statesman* wrote an editorial on her saying:

> It is not easy to explain the importance of Nargis .... Her most memorable quality was a rare combination of hard professionalism and quiet dignity. She represented a cinema, though wholly commercial, had little trace of crassness.

In Bombay glowing tributes were paid to her and the road in front of her Bandra home was named as Nargis Dutt Marg.[3]

NOTES

1. George, T.J.S., *The Life and Times of Nargis*, An Imprint of Harper Collins Publishers India, New Delhi, 1994.
2. Jain, C.K., *Women Parliamentarians in India*, Surjeet Publications, New Delhi, 1993.
3. Cour, Ajeet and Cour Arpana, (Ed.), *Directory of Indian Women Today: 1976*, India International Publications, New Delhi, 1976.

30

Smt. Mohsina Kidwai

Smt. Mohsina Kidwai was born on 1st January, 1932, in Banda district of Uttar Pradesh. Her father Qutubuddin Ahmad was a great supporter of education especially women's education. She studied upto the intermediate level and was by profession a social worker. She was married to Shri Khalilur Rahman Kidwai on 13th December, 1953. Later on she joined politics and held several important portfolios. In 1973-74 she was the Minister of State, Food and Civil Supplies, Government of Uttar Pradesh. In 1974-75 she was the Cabinet Minister, Harijan and Social Welfare, Government of Uttar Pradesh. In 1974-77 she was a member of Uttar Pradesh Legislative Assembly. In 1975-77 she became a Cabinet Minister of Small-Scale Industries of Government of Uttar Pradesh. In 1978 on Congress-I ticket she became a member of the sixth Lok Sabha. In 1976-80 she acquired the distinction of being the president of P.C.C. (Pradesh Congress Committee) of Uttar Pradesh. Similarly in 1980-84 she became the member of the seventh Lok Sabha. From 1982 to 1983 she became the Union Minister of State for Labour and Rehabilitation. Later from 1983 to 1984 she became the Union Minister of State for Health and Family Welfare. In 1984 she was elected to the eighth Lok Sabha as a Congress-I candidate from Meerut, Uttar Pradesh. In the same year she was appointed as the Union Minister of State (Independent Charge) for Rural Development. From 1984 to 1986 she was the Union Minister for Health and Family Welfare. From 1986 to 1989 she held two portfolios, i.e. Union Cabinet Minister for Transport and Cabinet Minister for Urban Development. In 1988 she held charge of Ministry of Tourism from 22nd October to 2nd December 1989.[1]

Mohsina took special interest in helping the poor and the destitute women and children. She was the founder patron of the National Girls' Higher Secondary School, Barabanki, Condensed Course School for promotion of literacy among adult women for making them self-supporting, Tailoring and Embroidery Centre for Women and Bal Jagat for providing shelter to the orphans and forsaken children and children belonging to the poor families.

She had travelled widely and was a member of the official delegation to U.S.A., U.K., Tanzania, Mauritius, Kenya and United Arab Emirates. She was also a member of the official delegation at the Women's Conference in German Democratic Republic and World Peace Conference, USSR, Brunei and Hungary.

NOTE

1. Jain, C.K., *Women Parliamentarians in India*, Surjeet Publications, New Delhi, 1993.

31

Conclusion

The history of medieval, modern and the contemporary periods have very rich accounts of few eminent Muslim women who were legend makers of their time. These women such as Razia Sultan, Nur Jahan, Jahan Ara, Begams of Bhopal, Nawab Faizunnessa, Rokeya Sakhawat Hossein, Masuma Begam, Rashid Jahan, Ismat Chughtai, Nargis, Begam Akbar Jehan and many more have left their marks in different fields. Their contributions and achievements which are graphically portrayed by them in their biographical works and sometimes by few scholars writing about them, gives an in-depth account of their trials and successes and the kind of impact their activities had on society and on women in particular.

The above mentioned women cannot be called as social rebels or feminists in the true sense of the term. The various activities undertaken by them was in harmony with the Islamic traditions. What they sought to do was to question those institutions, e.g. purdah and child-marriage that was responsible in keeping most of the Muslim women in seclusion, segregation, and devoid of any kind of formal education.

Like the male intelligentsia the Muslim women intelligentsia, belonging to different periods sought to improve the social status of Muslim women through their own personal examples, establishing formal institutions of learning, penning down their ideas in different forms of literary expressions, and establishing organization that took up social and educational issues.

The schools that were established by the educated Muslim *bhadramahila* perpetuated cultural continuity—for their emphasis was on those areas of curriculum which would enable girls to become good wives and mothers in their later lives. Further the curtains of purdah was not turn down by them, but was rather institutionalized. Schools that were established by the female intelligentsia saw to it that veiled carriages were provided to the girls while commuting from their homes to the schools. This was mainly done to ensure social acceptance of the schools that were established by them from the Muslim community, especially the orthodoxy.

Female schools that became prominent were especially established in the Bengal Presidency, the United Provinces and in the Princely State of Bhopal. Some of the well-known schools were the Sakhavat Memorial School in the Bengal Presidency and the Victoria and the Sultania School in the Princely State of Bhopal. The former was established by Sakhavat Husain and the latter was by the Begams of Bhopal.

Some of the educated women intelligentsia like the Begams of Bhopal encouraged professional education among women. The profession that became popular among Muslim girls was—teaching, mid-wifery and nursing.

Apart from establishing formal institutions most of the educated women of the above mentioned period were prolific writers. Some of them wrote their own biographical accounts, e.g. Nawab Sultan Jahan Begam wrote her biography—"An Account of My Life" in three volumes. These volumes were subsequently translated into English. Educated Muslim women also took up themes that centred around the daily life of women. In this connection Nawab Shah Jahan Begam of Bhopal wrote *Tahzib-un-Niswanwa Tarbiyat-al-Insan* (The Cultivation of Woman and the Instruction of Humanity). This manuscript contains chapters on—women and children's illnesses, pregnancy and child-birth, the education and socialization of children, prayer, fasting, purdah, marriage, divorce, death, and mourning, as well as household management, and she also patronized other texts for schools in her state, such as the Silsilah-i-Sultaniya (Sultaniya Series). These books especially the latter one was meant for classes in 'domestic economy' in schools.

Themes on social status of Muslim women in society were also penned by them in their writings. Rashid Jahan, the eldest daughter of Sheikh Abdullah of Aligarh wrote short stories on the position of women in the family and in the society. In fact, Rashid Jahan became a source of inspiration to Ismat Chughtai, who became one of the best known authors of modern Urdu short stories. Her book *Lihaf* (The Quilt) caused a lot of furor. It was mainly concerned with the wife's sexual frustration and her subsequent relationship with a female servant with whom she finds emotional and sexual companionship. The theme chosen by Ismat was unthinkable even for the progressive writers among the Muslims. She was prosecuted by the Punjab government for obscenity. Later the charges against her was dismissed. Similarly, Shaista Suhrawardy Ikramullah in her work "From Purdah to Parliament" gives a very graphic discussion of her journey from the private to the public sphere.

In an age when women organizations were not very popular, some educated Muslim women who belonged to the social reformist families established associations that took up social and educational issues. Some of the significant organizations that were established was *Anjuman-i-Khavatin-i-Islam* (All India Muslim Ladies Conference) in 1914. This organization claimed to speak for all the Muslim women of India. Despite, being the spokes person of all the Muslim women, its activities largely remained confined to the urban educated Muslim women. Some of the important agenda of the organization that were constantly discussed was—promoting women's education and enhancing the age of marriage.

The activities of Anjuman-i-Khavatin-i-Islam had certainly fostered on increased sense of community and social consciousness among Muslim women. It had definitely provided a respectable meeting place for purdah observing women from many provinces.

Some Muslim women also became members of the All India Women's Conference and took active part in its deliberations. Few Muslim women were also its office bearers, e.g. Begam Sharifa Hamid Ali and Masuma Begam.

Education and social consciousness among the urban Muslim women brought them closer to the freedom struggle. They actively participated as members of the Women's Indian Association that met Montagu on 1917 to ask for the franchise for women.[1]

In post-independent India the rich legacy of the contribution of Muslim women in different fields has continued. Muslim women parliamentarians, writers, artists find reference in the pages of contemporary textbooks, magazines and periodicals. Even though they are a handful and have tried to de-mystify the stereotypical image of Muslim women, i.e. invisible, unheard of, having no voice, living in purdah and in the zenana apartment of the household.

These legend makers who belong to different periods of history have become a source of inspiration and motivation to all women irrespective of their religion or caste. Perhaps their achievement has continued to motivate the enrolment of Muslim girls in formal institutions of learning.[2]

NOTES

1. A women deputation consisting of fourteen women leaders such as lady Abala Bose, Mrs. Mazural Huque, Mrs. Nehru, Mrs. Chandrasekhar Aiyar, Mrs. Lazarus, Mrs. Herabai Tata, Dr. Miss Joshi, Mrs. Sanjiva Rao, Miss Gokhale, Annie Besant, Dorothy Jinaragadasa and Mrs. Cousins under the leadership of Sarojini Naidu, waited on Montague at Madras for demanding suffrage right for women. For details see, Srivastava, Gouri, *Women's Higher Education in the 19th Century*, Concept Publishing Company, New Delhi, 2000.
2. Enrolment of Muslim girls at different levels of education is given in the Appendix.

APPENDICES

Appendix-I

POLICY FRAMEWORK, PLANS, EDUCATIONAL POLICY

Policy Framework

The Constitution of India grants the right to Equality and the Right to Freedom of Religion and Protection of Interests of Minorities in regard to cultural and educational rights. A number of constitutional provisions exists for protection and promotion of the interests of these minority groups.

Article 14 : Equality before law.

Article 29 : Any section of the citizens residing in the territory of India or any part thereof having a distinct language, script or culture of its own shall have the right to conserve the same.

No citizen shall be denied admission into any educational institution maintained by the State or recovering aid out of State funds on grounds only of religion, race, caste, language or any of them.

Article 30 : All minorities whether based on religion or language shall have right to establish and administer educational institutions of their own choice.

The State shall not in granting aid to educational institutions, discriminate against any educational institution on the ground that it is under the management of minority, whether based on religion on language.

Article 350 : It shall be the endeavour of every State and of every local authority within the State to provide adequate facilities for instruction in the mother tongue at the primary stage of education to children belonging to linguistic minority groups; and the President of India may issue such directions to any State as he/she considers necessary or proper for securing the provision of such facilities.

Article 340 : Appointment of Commission to investigate the conditions of socially and educationally backward classes.

Equalization of educational opportunities is one of the prime concerns of the Government since Independence. Government of India has launched many programmes as a part of the efforts of the equalisation of educational opportunities for the development of educationally backward minorities since Independence.

Smt. Indira Gandhi, the then Prime Minister of India had issued 15-point programme in 1983 for the welfare of the Minorities.

- Point 11 directs the State authorities to take steps for starting *coaching classes in minority educational institutions* for enabling minority students to compete successfully in admission and recruitment tests.
- Point 12 directs the States to make arrangement for setting up *community polytechnics* by Government or Private agencies in predominantly minority areas and to encourage admission in these institutions of persons belonging to the minority communities.

Plans

The Five Year Developmental Plans also specified the need for education of the Muslim Community.

The Ninth Five Year Plan emphasised that in spite of adequate facilities at secondary stage, children from minority groups were not taking full advantages of these. The scheme of Modernisation of Madrasas according to the plans would receive all possible attention, so as to cover more Madrasas and improve the access of Muslim children to education.

Area Intensive Programme would be strengthened by allocating a higher outlay. A vigorous publicity drive would be undertaken to generate necessary awareness among the Minority Communities so that they would come forward to take full advantage of the scheme. The cooperation of the leaders of the minority communities would be elicited for the fulfilment of the same objective.

Educational Policy

The National Policy on Education 1979 states: "The Government is aware of the valuable contribution of the country's composite culture that can be made by institutions run by religions and linguistic minorities and recognise and uphold their right to establish such educational institutions of their choice and administer them in accordance with law, in order that the goal of an integrated Indian Community is achieved." (NPE 1979, Ministry of Education and Social Welfare, GOI, p. 21).

The National Policy on Education 1968 : "Every effort should be made not only to protect the rights of minorities but to promote their educational interests as suggested in the statement issued by the Conference of the Chief Ministers of States and Central Ministries held in August 1961." (National Policy on Education, Ministry of Education and Social Welfare, GOI, 1974, pp. 8-9).

The National Policy on Education (NPE) and its Programme of Action (POA) 1986, as updated in 1992 envisages paying greater attention to the education of the educationally backward minorities in the interest of equity and social justice.

The NPE 1986 and revised 1992 states: "Some minority groups are educationally deprived or backward. Greater attention will be paid to the education of these groups in the interest of equality and social justice. This will naturally include the Constitutional guarantees given to them to establish and administer their own educational institutions, and protection to their languages and culture". (para 4.8)

The POA 1986 identified 41 educationally backward districts of Muslim population and also states the following measures for achieving the educational development of such minority groups.

— To encourage minority educational societies to establish new institutions and develop infrastructure in existing institutions. The government has also undertaken not only to recognize such societies and to assist them, but also to grant scholarship etc. through such societies to make them effective, responsive, and responsible.

— Imparting of technical skills through the 10 community polytechnics set up in areas of predominant minority concentrations.

— University Grants Commission's Scheme of giving assistance to universities/colleges for starting coaching classes for students belonging to educationally backward minorities.

In the remaining years of the VIIth Plan (1986-87 to 1989-90), the Programme of Action 1986 set the following four targets for the various minorities :

- Setting up of Resource Centres at Aligarh Muslim University, Jamia Millia Islamia, Kashmir University, Marathwada University and Osmania University at Hyderabad.
- Early Childhood Education Centres in the areas predominantly inhabited by educationally backward minorities.
- A number of decisions were taken in the Programme of Action for Primary, Middle and Higher Secondary Education, Vocational and Technical Education.
- Women's Education with regard to backward minorities: "As the women literacy and the girls enrolment is lowest among educationally backward minorities, in the scheme of opening of girls schools, appointment of lady teachers, opening of girls hostels and providing of incentives in the form of mid-day meals, uniforms etc. Minorities needs should be fully met. A production-cum-training centre for crafts exclusively for girls preferably with women instructors to the extent possible in each of the identified minority concentration districts. This will be done by State Governments."

In order to provide training and guidance to minority educational institution, the Programme of Action also contained long-term plans to teach Sciences, Mathematics and English on voluntary basis in institutions imparting in traditional schools.

The State Governments were asked to set up an institutionalized system for compilation of statistical information regarding educational facilities required by the Commissioner for Linguistic Minorities.

The group on minorities, SC, ST and other weaker sections appointed by Ministry of Home Affairs head by Dr. Gopal Singh has identified Muslims and Neo-Buddhists as educationally backward groups at the national level. Neo-Buddhists were given all the benefits which are available to Scheduled Castes and therefore, the Muslims are recognised as educationally backward minority group at the national level. The group on Minority Education set up by the Department of Education in 1990 has suggested area approach in school education. This has been recommended by the Empowered Committee also which was set up to take decisions on the report of the Group on minorities. Again, this has been endorsed by the Central Advisory Board of Education in its meeting held on 5-6 May, 1992 and the Task Force on Minorities Education constituted for formulating the New Programme of Action.

The Programme of Action 1992 realized the importance and necessity of voluntary efforts in the field, especially for opening of new schools in the minority areas. The State Governments were asked to formulate clear guidelines and recognition policy with regard to minority institutions and the same were to be given wide publicity. The disposal of applications should also be expeditious. The Programme of Action envisages setting up of Statewise Federation of Minority Institutions for effective implementation of educational uplift measures, for maintaining academic standards and minimum infrastructure facilities and for implementation of several measures in this programme. These bodies are to be officially recognised and supported.

Appendix-II

PERCENTAGE OF GIRLS ENROLMENT TO TOTAL ENROLMENT IN MUSLIM CONCENTRATION DISTRICTS OF INDIA

(as on 30 Sept. 1999)

Sl.	State/District	Enrolments Classes I-V			Enrolments Classes VI-VIII		
No.		Total	Girls	% Girls	Total	Girls	% Girls
	Uttar Pradesh						
1.	Bahraich	200113	56361	28.16	39381	9172	23.29
2.	Barabanki	236766	81342	34.36	57923	16001	27.62
3.	Basti	251795	84446	33.54	105439	25441	24.13
4.	Bijnor	235355	87390	37.13	76618	24305	31.72
5.	Deoria	423704	146068	34.47	119145	33696	28.28
6.	Ghaziabad	208611	88618	42.48	99260	47465	47.82
7.	Gonda	258965	73997	28.57	69581	14321	20.58
8.	Meerut	324840	136811	42.12	146691	53486	36.46
9.	Moradabad	—	—	—	—	—	—
10.	Muzaffarnagar	282375	108088	38.28	97439	33101	33.97
11.	Pillibhit	119855	39987	33.36	31326	7551	24.10
12.	Rampur	102151	30477	29.84	25586	7393	28.89
13.	Saharanpur	217418	82685	38.03	72153	24403	33.82
	West Bengal						
14.	Murshidabad	674914	327643	48.55	131705	49816	37.82
15.	Maldah	170069	359507	—	97185	36526	37.58
16.	West Dinajpur	226560	102244	45.13	58631	21055	35.91
17.	Birbhoom	377464	162332	43.01	101910	41207	40.43
18.	Nadia	480662	204171	42.48	185652	67020	36.10
19.	24-Parganas N	854779	404316	47.30	184307	87811	47.64
20.	24-Parganas S	857509	377041	43.97	206599	85489	41.38
21.	Kuch-Bihar	338440	152675	45.11	75126	31518	41.95
22.	Howrah	412708	194493	47.13	132973	57499	43.24

(Contd.)

(Contd.)

Sl. No.	State/District	Enrolments Classes I-V			Enrolments Classes VI-VIII		
		Total	Girls	% Girls	Total	Girls	% Girls
	Kerala						
23.	Kannanore	169132	82606	48.84	146350	70017	47.84
24.	Kozhikode	193894	93946	48.45	166965	80354	48.13
25.	Malappuram	321360	155989	48.54	264480	127312	48.14
26.	Palghat	184336	90434	49.06	155059	75016	48.38
27.	Wyanad	52037	25274	48.57	40384	19399	48.04
	Bihar						
28.	Darbhanga	350440	124237	35.45	64736	18922	29.23
29.	Katihar	69218	22710	32.81	33931	10173	29.98
30.	Purnea	187597	62879	33.52	34744	9203	26.49
	Karnataka						
31.	Bidar	N.A.	N.A.	N.A.	N.A.	N.A.	N.A.
32.	Bijapur	N.A.	N.A.	N.A.	N.A.	N.A.	N.A.
33.	Gulbarga	N.A.	N.A.	N.A.	N.A.	N.A.	N.A.
	Maharashtra						
34.	Greater Bombay	N.A.	N.A.	—	N.A.	N.A.	—
35.	Aurangabad	415715	192115	46.21	139472	57362	41.13
	Andhra Pradesh						
36.	Hyderabad	372109	189224	50.85	171892	88908	51.72
37.	Kurnool	486216	220766	45.40	100247	36795	36.70
	Haryana						
38.	Gurgaon	176819	75478	42.69	57824	23650	40.90
	M.P.						
39.	Bhopal	203900	94686	46.44	82708	37625	45.49
	Rajasthan						
40.	Jaisalmair	188200	49700	46.41	12900	3700	28.68
	Gujarat						
41.	Kachch	187248	79549	42.48	62784	25129	40.02

Source : State Department of Education, 2000 (unpublished data).

PERCENTAGE OF GIRLS ENROLMENT TO TOTAL ENROLMENT IN MUSLIM CONCENTRATION DISTRICTS OF INDIA

(as on 30 Sept. 1999)

Sl. No.	State/District	Enrolments Classes IX-X			Enrolments Classes XI-XII		
		Total	Girls	% Girls	Total	Girls	% Girls
	Uttar Pradesh						
1.	Bahraich	16810	3114	18.52	6221	1754	28.19
2.	Barabanki	20002	3129	15.64	5660	1325	23.41
3.	Basti	41134	7159	17.40	13628	2979	21.86
4.	Bijnor	33386	8279	24.80	15937	5454	34.22
5.	Deoria	57276	12032	21.01	21943	5456	24.86
6.	Ghaziabad	57215	19317	33.76	23891	10419	43.61
7.	Gonda	27285	4591	16.83	8598	2194	25.52
8.	Meerut	83262	57076	68.55	39551	15214	38.47
9.	Moradabad	—	—	—	—	—	—
10.	Muzaffarnagar	47705	13053	27.36	20539	7634	37.17
11.	Pillibhit	13061	2551	19.53	4099	1381	33.69
12.	Rampur	11439	3323	29.05	5236	1921	36.69
13.	Saharanpur	36399	10568	29.08	15187	6037	39.75
	West Bengal						
14.	Murshidabad	49251	14627	29.70	32100	6911	21.53
15.	Maldah	30554	9772	31.98	15360	3121	20.32
16.	West Dinajpur	14025	4044	28.83	8029	2222	27.67
17.	Birbhoom	30967	9384	30.30	16156	3424	21.19
18.	Nadia	76069	25238	33.18	36601	8669	23.69
19.	24-Parganas N	83221	25180	30.26	48645	11459	23.56
20.	24-Parganas S	63426	18883	29.77	32198	7571	23.51
21.	Kuch-Bihar	23974	7590	31.66	14000	4006	28.61
22.	Howrah	62627	19312	30.84	46149	10068	21.82
	Kerala						
23.	Kannanore	134788	67699	50.23	2558	1480	57.86
24.	Kozhikode	159608	80104	50.19	3674	1752	47.69
25.	Malappuram	222800	112520	50.50	2164	967	44.69

(Contd.)

Sl. No.	State/District	Enrolments Classes IX-X			Enrolments Classes XI-XII		
		Total	Girls	% Girls	Total	Girls	% Girls
26.	Palghat	140250	71501	50.98	2765	1284	46.44
27.	Wyanad	37479	19245	51.35	587	281	47.87
	Bihar						
28.	Darbhanga	23407	5965	25.48	127	7	5.51
29.	Katihar	12218	3453	28.26	474	281	59.28
30.	Purnea	10815	2039	18.85	166	43	25.90
	Karnataka						
31.	Bidar	N.A.	N.A.	N.A.	N.A.	N.A.	N.A.
32.	Bijapur	N.A.	N.A.	N.A.	N.A.	N.A.	N.A.
33.	Gulbarga	N.A.	N.A.	N.A.	N.A.	N.A.	N.A.
	Maharashtra						
34.	Greater Bombay	N.A.	N.A.	—	N.A.	N.A.	—
35.	Aurangabad	58919	23204	39.38	11503	4693	40.80
	Andhra Pradesh						
36.	Hyderabad	83262	43940	52.77	1267	639	50.43
37.	Kurnool	40516	14385	35.50	103	28	27.18
	Haryana						
38.	Gurgaon	22365	8581	38.37	12783	4956	38.77
	M.P.						
39.	Bhopal	31266	15457	49.44	25427	11997	47.18
	Rajasthan						
40.	Jaisalmair	3761	677	18.00	1886	348	18.45
	Gujarat						
41.	Kachch	22132	8446	38.16	7023	3318	47.24

Source : State Department of Education, 2000 (unpublished data).

Bibliography

Ali, Ashfaq Syed, *A Guide to Bhopal*, Jai Bharat Publishing House, Bhopal, 1987.

Banerji, S.K., *Humayun Badshah*, Vol. II, Maxwell Company, Lucknow, 1941.

Basu, Aparna and Ray, Nandita, Jerry Nara Sunhan, Diamond Jubilee, 1927-87, All India Womens' Conference, New Delhi, Mahila Press (A.I.W.C.), New Delhi, 1987.

Cour, Ajeet and Cour Arpana, (Ed.), *Directory of Indian Women Today*: 1976, India International Publications, New Delhi, 1976.

George, T.J.S., *The Life and Times of Nargis*, An Imprint of Harper Collins Publishers India, New Delhi, 1994.

Jain, C.K., *Women Parliamentarians in India*, Surjeet Publications, New Delhi, 1993.

Madhavananda, Swami, Majumdar, Ramesh Chandra, *Great Women of India*, Published by Swami Ananyananda, President, Advaita Ashrama, Mayavati Pithoragarh, Himalayas, Calcutta, 1982.

Minault, Gail, *Secluded Scholars: Women's Education and Muslim Social Reform in Colonial India*, Oxford University Press, New Delhi, 1998.

Mittal, Kamla, *History of Bhopal State: Development of Constitution, Administration and National Awakening 1901-1949*, Munshiram Manoharlal Publishers Pvt. Ltd., New Delhi, 1990.

Nath, Renuka, *Notable Mughal and Hindu Women in the 16th and 17th Centuries A.D.*, Inter-India Publications, New Delhi, 1990.

Nizami, Khaliq Ahmad, *Some Aspects of Religion and Politics in India During the Thirteenth Century*, Idarah-I-Ababiyat-i-Delhi, Delhi, 1978.

Prasad, Beni, *History of Jahangir*, Fifth Edition, The Indian Press (Publication) Pvt. Ltd., Allahabad, 1962.

Preckel, Claudia, *Begums of Bhopal*, Lotus Collections Roli Books, New Delhi, 2000.

Rawat, P.L., *History of Indian Education*.

Ray, Bharati (Ed.), *From The Seams of History: Essays on Indian Women*, Oxford University Press, New Delhi, 1995.

Shah Jahan Begam, Nawab, *Taj-ul-Ikbal Tarikh Bhopal;* or *The History of Bhopal*, Trans. H.C. Barstow, Calcutta, 1876.

Srivastava, A.L., *History of India (1000-1707 A.D.),* Shiva Lal Agarwala & Company, Educational Publishers, Agra.

Srivastava, Gouri, *Women Who Created History*, NCERT, New Delhi, 1997.

Sultan Jahan Begam, *An Account of My Life: Gohur-i-Iqbal*, Vol. I, Vol. II. Vol. I translated by C.H. Payne, London: Murray, 1912. Vol. II translated by Abdus Samad Khan, Bombay, 1922.

_______, Hayat-i-Qudsia: *Life of Nawab Gauhar Begam alias the Nawab Begam Qudsia of Bhopal*. Trans. W.S. Davis, London, 1918.

_______, *Hayat-i-Shahjahani: Life of Her Higheness : the Late Nawab Shahjahan Begum of Bhopal*, translated by B. Ghosal, Bombay, 1926.

News Papers/Magazines

- *Hindustan Times*
- *The Times of India*
- *Nation and the World*

INDEX